Oedipus at

Kolonos

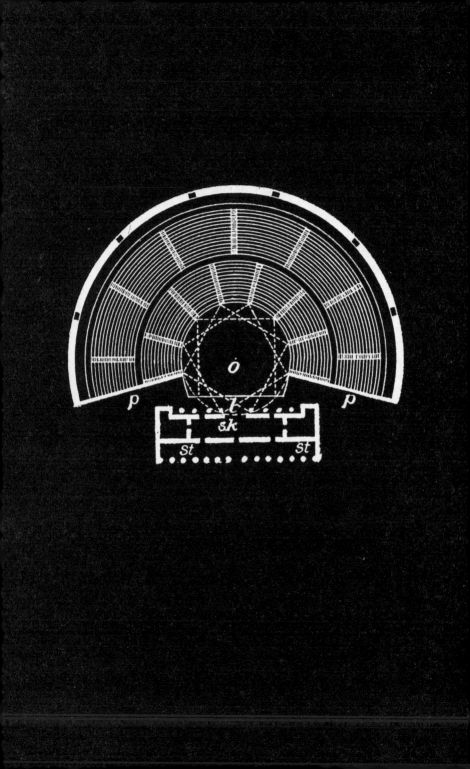

OEDIPUS AT KOLONOS

A New Translation by Robert Bagg

SOPHOCLES

HARPER ● PERENNIAL

NEW YORK ● LONDON ● TORONTO ● SYDNEY ● NEW DELHI ● AUCKLAND

HARPER ● PERENNIAL

For performance rights to *Oedipus at Kolonos* contact The Strothman Agency, LLC, at 197 Eighth Street, Flagship Wharf – 611, Charlestown, MA 02129, or by email at info@strothmanagency.com.

HarperCollins books may be purchased for educational, business, or sales promotional use. For information please write: Special Markets Department, HarperCollins Publishers, 10 East 53rd Street, New York, NY 10022.

FIRST EDITION

Designed by Justin Dodd

Library of Congress Cataloging-in-Publication Data is available upon request.

ISBN 978-0-06-213210-9

12 13 14 15 16 /RRD 10 9 8 7 6 5 4 3 2 1

For Mary Bagg, who was at my side
on the much-traveled and eventful road that took us from bloody Thebes
through shining Kolonos to welcoming Athens

CONTENTS

WHEN THEATER WAS LIFE: THE WORLD OF SOPHOCLES

I

Greek theater emerged from the same explosive creativity that propelled the institutions and ways of knowing of ancient Athens, through two and a half millennia, into our own era. These ranged from the concept and practice of democracy, to an aggressive use of logic with few holds barred, to a philosophy singing not of gods and heroes but of what exists, where it came from, and why. Athenians distinguished history from myth, acutely observed the human form, and reconceived medicine from a set of beliefs and untheorized practices into a science.

Playwrights, whose work was presented to audiences of thousands, effectively took center stage as critics and interpreters of their own culture. Athenian drama had one major showing each year at the nine-day Festival of Dionysos. It was rigorously vetted. Eight dramatists (three tragedians, five comic playwrights), chosen in open competition, were "granted choruses," a down-to-earth term meaning that the city financed production of their plays. For the Athenians theater was as central to civic life as the assembly, law courts, temples, and agora.

Historians summing up Athens' cultural importance have tended to emphasize its glories, attending less to the brutal institutions and policies that underwrote the city's wealth and dominance: its slaves, for instance, who worked the mines that enriched the communal treasury; or its policy of executing the men and enslaving the women and children of enemy cities that refused to surrender on demand. During its long war with Sparta, Athens' raw and unbridled democracy became increasingly reckless, cruel, and eventually self-defeating. Outside the assembly's daily debates on war, peace, and myriad other issues, Athenian citizens, most notably the indefatigable Socrates, waged ongoing critiques of the city's actions and principles. Playwrights, whom the Athenians called *didaskaloi* (educators), were expected to enlighten audiences about themselves, both individually and collectively. As evidenced by the thirty-three plays that survive, these works presented a huge audience annually with conflicts and dilemmas of the most extreme sort.

To some extent all Sophocles' plays engage personal, social, and political crises and confrontations—not just those preserved in heroic legend but those taking place in his immediate world. Other Athenian intellectuals, including Thucydides, Aeschylus, Euripides, Plato, and Aristophanes, were part of that open-ended discussion in which everything was subject to question, including the viability of the city and its democracy (which was twice voted temporarily out of existence).

II

To this day virtually every Athenian theatrical innovation—from paraphernalia such as scenery, costumes, and masks to the architecture of stage and seating and, not least, to the use of drama as a powerful means of cultural and political commentary—remains in use. We thus inherit from Athens the vital *potential* for drama to engage our realities and to support or critique prevailing orthodoxies.

The myths that engaged Sophocles' audience originated in Homer's epics of the Trojan War and its aftermath. Yet Homer's world was tribal. That of the Greek tragedians was not, or only nominally so. With few exceptions (e.g., Aeschylus' *The Persians*), those playwrights were writing *through* the Homeric world to address, and deal with, the *polis* world they themselves were living in. Sophocles was appropriating stories and situations from these epics, which were central to the mythos of Athenian culture, and re-visioning them into dramatic *agons* (contests) relevant to the tumultuous, often vicious politics of Greek life in the fifth century BCE. Today some of Sophocles' concerns, and the way he approached them, correspond at their deepest levels to events and patterns of thought and conduct that trouble our own time. For example, "[Sophocles'] was an age when war was endemic. And Athens in the late fifth century BC appeared to have a heightened taste for conflict. One year of two in the Democratic Assembly, Athenian citizens voted in favor of military aggression" (Hughes, 138).

Each generation interprets and translates these plays in keeping with the style and idiom it believes best suited for tragedy.

Inevitably even the most skilled at preserving the original's essentials, while attuning its voice to the present, will eventually seem the relic of a bygone age. We have assumed that a contemporary translation should attempt to convey not only what the original seems to have been communicating, but *how* it communicated—not in its saying, only, but in its *doing*. It cannot be said too often: these plays were social and historical *events* witnessed by thousands in a context and setting infused with religious ritual and civic protocol. They were not transitory, one-off entertainments but were preserved, memorized, and invoked. Respecting this basic circumstance will not guarantee a successful translation, but it is a precondition for giving these works breathing room in which their strangeness, their rootedness in distinct historical moments, can flourish. As with life itself, they were not made of words alone.

Athenian playwrights relied on a settled progression of scene types: usually a prologue followed by conversations or exchanges in which situations and attitudes are introduced, then a series of confrontations that feature cut-and-thrust dialogue interrupted by messenger narratives, communal songs of exultation or grieving, and less emotionally saturated, or 'objective,' choral odes that respond to or glance off the action. Audiences expected chorus members to be capable of conveying the extraordinary range of expressive modes, from the pithy to the operatic, that Sophocles had at his disposal. To translate this we have needed the resources not only of idiomatic English but also of rhetorical gravitas and, on occasion, colloquial English. Which is why we have adopted, regarding vocabulary and 'levels of speech,' a wide and varied palette. When Philoktetes

exclaims, "You said it, boy," that saying corresponds in character to the colloquial Greek expression. On the other hand Aias's
"Long rolling waves of time . . ." is as elevated, without being
pompous, as anything can be.

Unfortunately we've been taught, and have learned to live
with, washed-out stereotypes of the life and art of 'classical'
times—just as we have come to associate Greek sculpture with
the color of its underlying material, usually white marble. The
classical historian Bettany Hughes writes in *The Hemlock Cup*
(81) that temples and monuments were painted or stained in
"Technicolor" to be seen under the bright Attic sun. The stat-
ues' eyes were not blanks gazing off into space. They had color:
a *look*. To restore their flesh tones, their eye color, and the
bright hues of their cloaks would seem a desecration. We should
understand that this is so—even as we recognize that, for us,
there is no going back. We've been conditioned to preserve not
the reality of ancient Greek sculpture in its robust cultural am-
bience and physical setting, but our own fixed conception of it
as colorless and sedate—a perception created, ironically, by the
weathering and ravages of centuries. No one can change that.
Still, as translators we have a responsibility not to reissue a ste-
reotype of classical Greek culture but rather to recoup, to the
extent possible, the vitality of its once living reality.

Regarding its highly inflected language, so different from our
more context-driven modern English, we recognize that locu-
tions sounding contorted, coy, recondite, or annoyingly round-
about were a feature of ordinary Greek and were intensified in
theatrical discourse. Highly wrought, larger-than-life expressions, delivered without artificial amplification to an audience

of thousands, did not jar when resonating in the vast Theater of Dionysos, but may to our own Anglophone ears when delivered from our more intimate stages and screens, or read in our books and electronic tablets. Accordingly, where appropriate, and especially in rapid exchanges, we have our characters speak more straightforwardly—as happens in Greek stichomythia, when characters argue back and forth in alternating lines (or 'rows') of verse, usually linked by a word they hold in common. Here, for example, is a snippet from *Aias* (1305–1309)[1] that pivots on "right," "killer," "dead" and "god(s)":

TEUKROS   A righteous cause is my courage.
MENELAOS What? It's right to defend my killer?
TEUKROS   Your killer!? You're dead? And still alive?
MENELAOS A god saved me. But he *wanted* me dead.
TEUKROS   If the gods saved you, why disrespect them?

There are no rules for determining when a more-literal or less-literal approach is appropriate. Historical and dramatic context have to be taken into account. The objective is not only to render the textual meaning (which is ordinarily more on the phrase-by-phrase than the word-by-word level) but also to communicate the feel and impact embedded in that meaning. Dictionaries are indispensable for translators, but they are not sufficient. The meanings of words are immeasurably more nuanced and wide-ranging in life than they can ever be in a lexicon. As in life, where most 'sayings' cannot be fully grasped apart from their timing and their place in both personal and social contexts, so in theater: dramatic context must take words up and finish them off. In *Aias*, Teukros, the out-of-wedlock half brother of Aias, and Menelaos, co-commander of the Greek forces, are trading insults. When Menelaos says, "The archer, far from blood dust, thinks he's something," Teukros quietly rejoins, "I'm very good at what I do" (1300–1301).

Understanding the exchange between the two men requires that the reader or audience recognize the 'class' implications of archery. Socially and militarily, archers rank low in the pecking order. They stand to the rear of the battle formation. Archers are archers usually because they can't afford the armor one needs to be a hoplite, a frontline fighter. The point is that Teukros refuses to accept 'his place' in the social and military order. For a Greek audience, the sheer fact of standing his ground against a commander had to have been audacious. But that is not how it automatically registers in most modern word-by-word translations, which tend to make Teukros sound defensive (a trait wholly out of his character in this play). Examples: (a) "Even so, 'tis no sordid craft that I possess," (b) "I'm not the master of a menial skill," (c) "My archery is no contemptible science," (d) "The art I practice is no mean one." These translations are technically accurate. They're scrupulous in reproducing the Greek construction whereby, in an idiomatic context, a negative may register as an assertion—or even, framed as a negative future question, become a command. But tonally, in modern English idiom, Teukros' negation undercuts his assertion (the 'I'm not . . . but even so' formula). To our ears it admits weakness or defensiveness. "I'm very good at what I do," however, is a barely veiled threat. The dramatic arc of the encounter, which confirms that Teukros will not back down for anything or anyone, not even a commander of the Greek army, substantiates that Sophocles meant it to be heard as such.

Hearing the line in context we realize instantly not only what the words are saying but, more pointedly and feelingly, what they're doing. His words are not just 'about' something. They are an act in themselves—not, as in the more literal translations, a duress-driven apologia. Translation must thus respond to an individual character's ever-changing demeanor and circumstance. The speaker's state of mind should show through his or her words, just as in life. Idiomatic or colloquial expressions fit many situations better—especially those that have a more finely tuned emotional economy—than phrases that, if uninhabited, hollowed out, or just plain buttoned-up, sound evasive or euphemistic. Many of the speeches Sophocles gives his characters are as abrupt and common as he might himself have spoken to his fellow Athenians in the assembly, in the agora, to his troops, his actors, or his family.

At times we have chosen a more literal translation in passages where scholars have opted for a seemingly more accessible modern phrase. At the climactic moment in *Oedipus the King*, when Oedipus realizes he has killed his father and fathered children with his mother, he says in a modern prose version by Hugh Lloyd-Jones: "Oh, oh! All is now clear. O light, may I now look on you for the last time, I who am revealed as cursed in my birth, cursed in my marriage, cursed in my killing!" (Greek 1182–1885). When Lloyd-Jones uses and repeats the word "cursed," he is compressing a longer Greek phrase meaning "being shown to have done what must not be done." This compression shifts the emphasis from his unsuspecting human

actions toward the realm of the god who acted to "curse" him.
The following lines keep the original grammatical construction:

> All! All! It has all happened!
> It was all true. O light! Let this
> be the last time I look on you.
> You see now who I am—
> the child who must not be born!
> I loved where I must not love!
> I killed where I must not kill! (1336–1342)

Here Oedipus names the three acts of interfamilial trans-
gression that it was both his good and his ill fortune to have
survived, participated in, and inflicted—birth, sexual love, and
murder in self-defense—focusing not only on the curse each act
has become but now realizing the full and horrific consequence
of each action that was, as it happened, unknowable. Register-
ing the shudder rushing through him, Oedipus's exclamations
convey the shock of his realization: *I did these things without
feeling their horror as I do now.*

Finally, translations tend to be more or less effective depending on their ability to convey the emotional and physiological
reactions that will give a reader or an audience a kinesthetic re-
lationship to the dramatic moment, whether realized as text or
performance. This is a precondition for maintaining the tactil-
ity that characterizes any living language. Dante wrote that the
spirit of poetry abounds "in the tangled constructions and de-
fective pronunciations" of vernacular speech where language is
renewed and transformed. We have not attempted that—these

are translations, not new works—but we have striven for a language that is spontaneous and generative as opposed to one that is studied and bodiless. We have also worked to preserve the root meaning of Sophocles' Greek, especially his always illuminating metaphors.

III

Sophocles reveals several recurrent attitudes in his plays—sympathy for fate's victims, hostility toward leaders who abuse their power, skepticism toward self-indulgent 'heroes,' disillusionment with war and revenge—that are both personal and politically significant. All his plays to a greater or lesser degree focus on outcasts from their communities. Historically, those who transgress a community's values have either been physically exiled or stigmatized by sanctions and/or shunning. To keep a polity from breaking apart, everyone, regardless of social standing, must abide by certain enforceable communal expectations. Athens in the fifth century BCE practiced political ostracism, a procedure incorporated in its laws. By voting to ostracize a citizen, Athens withdrew its protection and civic benefits—sometimes to punish an offender, but also as a kind of referee's move, expelling a divisive public figure from the city (and from his antagonists) so as to promote a ten-year period of relative peace.

In earlier eras Greek cities also cast out those who committed sacrilege. Murderers of kin, for instance, or blasphemers of a god—in myth and in real life—were banished from Greek cities until the 'unclean' individual 'purged' his crime according to current religious custom. The imperative to banish a kin violator runs so deep that Oedipus, after discovering he has committed patricide and incest, passes judgment on himself and demands to live in exile. In *Oedipus at Kolonos*, he and Antigone have been exiled from Thebes against their will. In the non-Oedipus plays the title characters Philoktetes, Elektra, and Aias, as well as Herakles in *Women of Trakhis*, are not outcasts in the traditional sense, though all have actively or involuntarily offended their social units in some way. They may or may not be typical tragic characters; nonetheless none 'fit' the world they're given to live in. In these translations we've incorporated awareness of social dimensions in the original texts, which, as they involve exercises of power, are no less political than social.

In each of the four non-Oedipus plays, a lethal confrontation or conflict 'crazes' the surface coherence of a society (presumed to be Athenian society, either in itself or as mediated through a military context), thus revealing and heightening its internal contradictions.

In *Women of Trakhis* the revered hero Herakles, when he tries to impose a young concubine on his wife Deianeira, provokes her to desperate measures that unwittingly cause him horrific pain, whereupon he exposes his savage and egomaniacal nature, lashing out at everyone around him, exercising a hero's prerogatives so savagely that he darkens his own reputation and drives his wife to suicide and his son to bitter resentment.

Elektra exposes the dehumanizing cost of taking revenge, by revealing the neurotic, materialistic, and cold-blooded character of the avengers. In *Aias*, when the Greek Army's most powerful soldier tries to assassinate his commanders, whose authority rests on dubious grounds, he exposes not only them but his own growing obsolescence in a prolonged war that has more need of strategic acumen, as exemplified by Odysseus, than brute force. In *Philoktetes* the title character, abandoned on a deserted island because of a stinking wound his fellow warriors can't live with, is recalled to active service with the promise of a cure and rehabilitation. The army needs him and his bow to win the war. It is a call he resists, until the god Herakles negotiates a resolution—not in the name of justice, but because Philoktetes' compliance is culturally mandated. As in *Aias*, the object is to maintain the integrity and thus the survival of the society itself. The greatest threat is not an individual's death, which here is not the preeminent concern, but the disintegration of a society.

In our own time aspects of *Aias* and *Philoktetes* have been used for purposes that Sophocles, who was the sponsor in Athens of a healing cult, might have appreciated. Both heroes, but especially Aias, have been appropriated as exemplars of posttraumatic stress disorder, in particular as suffered by soldiers in and out of a war zone. Excerpts from these two plays have been performed around the United States for veterans, soldiers on active duty, their families, and concerned others. Ultimately, however, Sophocles is intent on engaging and resolving internal contradictions that threaten the historical continuity, the very future, of the Athenian city-state. He invokes the class contradictions Athens was experiencing by applying them to the mythical/historical eras from which he draws his plots.

Modern-day relevancies implicit in Sophocles' plays will come sharply into focus or recede from view depending on time and circumstance. The constant factors in these plays will always be their consummate poetry, dramatic propulsion, and the intensity with which they illuminate human motivation and morality. Scholars have also identified allusions in his plays to events in Athenian history. The plague in *Oedipus the King* is described in detail so vivid it dovetails in many respects with Thucydides' more clinical account of the plague that killed one-third to one-half of Athens' population beginning in 429 BCE. Kreon, Antigone's antagonist, displays the imperviousness to rational advice and lack of foresight exhibited by the politicians of Sophocles' era, whose follies Thucydides narrates, and which Sophocles himself was called in to help repair—specifically by taking a democracy that in a fit of imperial overreach suffered, in 413, a catastrophic defeat on the shores of Sicily, and replacing it with a revanchist oligarchy. When Pisander, one of the newly empowered oligarchs, asked Sophocles if he was one of the councilors who had approved the replacement of the democratic assembly by what was, in effect, a junta of four hundred, Sophocles admitted that he had. "Why?" asked Pisander. "Did you not think this a terrible decision?" Sophocles agreed it was. "So weren't you doing something terrible?" "That's right. There was no better alternative." (Aristotle, Rh. 1419a). The lesson? When life, more brutally than drama, delivers its irreversible calamities and judgments, it forces a polity, most movingly, to an utterly unanticipated, wholly 'other' moral and spiritual level.

In *Oedipus at Kolonos* Sophocles alludes to his city's decline when he celebrates a self-confident Athens that no longer existed when Sophocles wrote that play. He gives us Theseus, a throwback to the type of thoughtful, decisive, all-around leader Athens lacked as it pursued policies that left it impoverished

and defenseless—this under the delusion that its only enemies
were Spartans and Sparta's allies.

IV

Archaeologists have identified scores of local theaters all over
the Greek world—stone semicircles, some in cities and at religious destinations, others in rural villages. Within many of
these structures both ancient and modern plays are still staged.
Hillsides whose slopes were wide and gentle enough to seat a
crowd made perfect settings for dramatic encounters and were
the earliest theaters. Ancient roads that widened below a gentle
hillside, or level ground at a hill's base, provided suitable performance spaces. Such sites, along with every city's agora and
a temple dedicated to Dionysos or another god, were the main
arenas of community activity. Stone tablets along roads leading
to theaters commemorated local victors: athletes, actors, playwrights, singers, and the winning plays' producers. Theaters,
in every sense, were open to all the crosscurrents of civic and
domestic life.

The components of the earliest theaters reflect their rural
origins and were later incorporated into urban settings. *The-
atron*, the root of our word "theater," translates as "viewing
place" and designated the curved and banked seating area.
Orchestra was literally "the place for dancing." The costumed
actors emerged from and retired to the *skenê*, a word that originally meant, and literally was in the rural theaters, a tent. As
theaters evolved to become more permanent structures, the
skenê developed as well into a "stage building" whose painted

facade changed, like a mask, with the characters' various habitats. Depending on the drama, the *skenê* could assume the appearance of a king's grand palace, the Kyklops' cave, a temple to a god, or (reverting to its original material form) an army commander's tent.

Greek drama itself originated in two earlier traditions, one rural, one civic. Choral singing of hymns to honor Dionysos or other gods and heroes, which had begun in the countryside, evolved into the structured choral ode. The costumes and the dancing of choral singers, often accompanied by a reed instrument, are depicted on sixth-century vases that predate the plays staged in the Athenian theater. The highly confrontational nature of every play suggests how early choral odes and dialogues came into being in concert with a fundamental aspect of democratic governance: public and spirited debate. Two or more characters facing off in front of an audience was a situation at the heart of both drama and democratic politics.

Debate, the democratic Athenian art practiced and perfected by politicians, litigators, and thespians—relished and judged by voters, juries, and audiences—flourished in theatrical venues and permeated daily Athenian life. Thucydides used it to narrate his history of the war between Athens and Sparta. He recalled scores of lengthy debates that laid out the motives of politicians, generals, and diplomats as each argued his case for a particular policy or a strategy. Plato, recognizing the open-ended, exploratory power of spirited dialogue, wrote his philosophy entirely in dramatic form.

The Greeks were addicted to contests and turned virtually every chance for determining a winner into a formal competition. The Great Dionysia for playwrights and choral singers and the Olympics for athletes are only the most famous and familiar. The verbal *agon* remains to this day a powerful medium for testing and judging issues. And character, as in the debate between Teukros and Menelaos, may be laid bare. But there is no guarantee. Persuasiveness can be, and frequently is, manipulative (e.g., many of the sophists evolved into hired rhetorical guns, as distinguished from the truth-seeking, pre-Socratic philosophers). Sophocles may well have had the sophists' amorality in mind when he had Odysseus persuade Neoptomolos that betraying Philoktetes would be a patriotic act and bring the young man fame.

Though they were part of a high-stakes competition, the plays performed at the Dionysia were part of a religious ceremony whose chief purpose was to honor theater's patron god, Dionysos. The god's worshippers believed that Dionysos' powers and rituals transformed the ways in which they experienced and dealt with their world—from their enthralled response to theatrical illusion and disguise to the exhilaration, liberation, and violence induced by wine. Yet the festival also aired, or licensed, civic issues that might otherwise have had no truly public, *polis*-wide expression. The playwrights wrote as *politai*, civic poets, as distinguished from those who focused on personal lyrics and shorter choral works. Though *Aias* and *Philoktetes* are set in a military milieu, the issues they engage are essentially civil and political. Neither *Aias* nor *Philoktetes* is concerned with the 'enemy of record,' Troy, but rather with Greek-on-Greek conflict. With civil disruption, and worse. In fact one need look no further than the play venue itself for confirmation of the interpenetration of the civic with the military—a concern bordering on preoccupation—when, every year, the orphans of warriors killed in battle were given new hoplite armor and a place of honor at the Festival of Dionysos.

Communal cohesiveness and the historical continuity of the polity are most tellingly threatened from within: in *Aias* by the individualistic imbalance and arrogance of Aias, whose warrior qualities and strengths are also his weakness—they lead him to destroy the war spoil that is the common property of the entire Greek army—and in *Philoktetes* by the understandable and just, yet inordinately unyielding, self-preoccupation of Philoktetes himself. In both cases the fundamental, encompassing question is this: With what understandings, what basic values, is the commonality of the *polis* to be recovered and rededicated in an era in which civic cohesiveness is under the extreme pressure of a war Athens is losing (especially at the time *Philoktetes* was produced) and, further, the simmering stasis of unresolved class or caste interests? In sharply different ways, all three plays of the Oedipus cycle, as well as *Aias* and *Elektra*, cast doubt on the legitimacy of usurped, authoritarian, or publicly disapproved leadership.

Given the historical and political dynamism of these great, instructive works, we've aimed to translate and communicate their challenge to Athenian values for a contemporary audience whose own values are no less under duress.

V

The Great Dionysia was the central and most widely attended event of the political year, scheduled after winter storms had abated so that foreign visitors could come and bear witness to Athens' wealth, civic pride, imperial power, and artistic imagination. For eight or nine days each spring, during the heyday of Greek theater in the fifth century BCE, Athenians flocked to the temple grounds sacred to Dionysos on the southern slope of the Acropolis. After dark on the first day, a parade of young men hefted a giant phallic icon of the god from the temple and into the nearby theater. As the icon had been festooned with garlands of ivy and a mask of the god's leering face, their raucous procession initiated a dramatic festival called the City Dionysia, a name that differentiated it from the festival's ancient rural origins in Dionysian myth and cult celebrations of the god. As the festival gained importance in the sixth century BCE, most likely through the policies of Pisistratus, it was also known as the Great Dionysia.

Pisistratus, an Athenian tyrant in power off and on beginning in 561 BCE and continuously from 546 to 527, had good reason for adapting the Rural Dionysia as Athens' Great Dionysia: "Dionysos was a god for the 'whole' of democratic Athens" (Hughes, 213). Everyone, regardless of political faction or social standing, could relate to the boisterous communal activities of the festival honoring Dionysos: feasting, wine drinking, dancing, singing, romping through the countryside, and performing or witnessing dithyrambs and more elaborate dramatic works. The Great Dionysia thus served to keep in check, if not transcend, internal factionalizing by giving all citizens a 'natural' stake in Athens—Athens not simply as a place but as a venerable polity with ancient cultural roots. To this end Pisistratus had imported from Eleutherai an ancient phallic representation of Dionysos, one that took several men to carry.

Lodged as it was in a temple on the outskirts of Athens, this bigger-than-life icon gave the relatively new, citified cult the sanctified air of hoary antiquity (Csapo and Slater, 103–104). Thus validated culturally, the Great Dionysia was secured as a host to reassert, and annually rededicate, Athens as a democratic polity. As Bettany Hughes notes in *The Hemlock Cup*, "to call Greek drama an 'art-form' is somewhat anachronistic. The Greeks (unlike many modern-day bureaucrats) didn't distinguish drama as 'art'—something separate from 'society,' 'politics,' [or] 'life.' Theater was fundamental to democratic Athenian business. . . . [In] the fifth century this was the place where Athenian democrats came to understand the very world they lived in" (Hughes, 213).

The occasion offered Athens the chance to display treasure exacted from subjugated 'allies' (or tributes others willingly brought to the stage) and to award gold crowns to citizens whose achievements Athens' leaders wished to honor. Theater attendance itself was closely linked to citizenship; local town councils issued free festival passes to citizens in good standing. The ten generals elected yearly to conduct Athens' military campaigns poured libations to Dionysos. The theater's bowl seethed with a heady, sometimes unruly brew of military, political, and religious energy.

Performances began at dawn and lasted well into the

afternoon. The 14,000 or more Athenians present watched in god knows what state of anticipation or anxiety. Whatever else it did to entertain, move, and awe, Athenian tragedy consistently exposed human vulnerability to the gods' malice and favoritism. Because the gods were potent realities to Athenian audiences, they craved and expected an overwhelming emotional, physically distressing experience. That expectation distinguishes the greater intensity with which Athenians responded to plays from our own less challenging, more routine and frequent encounters with drama. Athenians wept while watching deities punish the innocent or unlucky, a reaction that distressed Plato. In his *Republic*, rather than question the motives or morality of the all-powerful Olympian gods for causing mortals grief, he blamed the poets and playwrights for their unwarranted wringing of the audience's emotions. He held that the gods had no responsibility for human suffering. True to form, Plato banned both poets and playwrights from his ideal city.

Modern audiences would be thoroughly at home with other, more cinematic stage effects. The sights and sounds tragedy delivered in the Theater of Dionysos were often spectacular. Aristotle, who witnessed a lifetime of productions in the fourth century—well after Sophocles' own lifetime, when the plays were performed in the heat of their historical moment—identified "spectacle," or *opsis*, as one of the basic (though to him suspect) elements of tragic theater. Under the influence of Aristotle, who preferred the study to the stage, and who therefore emphasized the poetry rather than the production of works, ancient commentators tended to consider "the visual aspects of drama [as] both vulgar and archaic" (Csapo and Slater, 257).

Nonetheless, visual and aural aspects there were: oboe music; dancing and the singing of set-piece odes by a chorus; masks that transformed the same male actor, for instance, into a swarthy-faced young hero, a dignified matron, Argos with a hundred eyes, or the Kyklops with only one. The theater featured painted scenery and large-scale constructions engineered with sliding platforms and towering cranes. It's hardly surprising that Greek tragedy has been considered a forerunner of Italian opera.

Judges awarding prizes at the Great Dionysia were chosen by lot from a list supplied by the council—one judge from each of Athens' ten tribes. Critical acumen was not required to get one's name on the list, but the *choregoi* (the producers and financial sponsors of the plays) were present when the jury was assembled and probably had a hand in its selection. At the conclusion of the festival the ten selected judges, each having sworn that he hadn't been bribed or unduly influenced, would inscribe on a tablet the names of the three competing playwrights in descending order of merit. The rest of the process depended on chance. The ten judges placed their ballots in a large urn. The presiding official drew five at random, counted up the weighted vote totals, and declared the winner.

VI

When Sophocles was a boy, masters trained him to excel in music, dance, and wrestling. He won crowns competing against his age-mates in all three disciplines. Tradition has it that he first appeared in Athenian national life at age fifteen, dancing naked (according to one source) and leading other boy dancers

in a hymn of gratitude to celebrate Athens' defeat of the Persian
fleet in the straits of Salamis.

Sophocles' father, Sophroniscus, manufactured weapons
and armor (probably in a factory operated by slaves), and his
mother, Phaenarete, was a midwife. The family lived in Kolonos, a rural suburb just north of Athens. Although his parents
were not aristocrats, as most other playwrights' were, they
surely had money and owned property; thus their status did not
hamper their son's career prospects. Sophocles' talents as a dra-
matist, so formidable and so precociously developed, won him
early fame. As an actor he triumphed in his own now-lost play,
Nausicaä, in the role of the eponymous young princess who
discovers the nearly naked Odysseus washed up on the beach
while playing ball with her girlfriends.

During Sophocles' sixty-five-year career as a *didaskalos*
he wrote and directed more than 120 plays and was awarded
first prize at least eighteen times. No record exists of his placing lower than second. Of the seven entire works of his that
survive, along with a substantial fragment of a satyr play, *The
Trackers*, only two very late plays can be given exact production
dates: *Philoktetes* in 409 and *Oedipus at Kolonos,* staged posthumously in 401. Some evidence suggests that *Antigone* was
produced around 442–441 and *Oedipus the King* in the 420s.
Aias, Elektra, and *Women of Trakhis* have been conjecturally,
but never conclusively, dated through stylistic analysis. Aristotle, who had access we forever lack to the hundreds of fifth-
century plays produced at the Dionysia, preferred Sophocles
to his rivals Aeschylus and Euripides. He considered *Oedipus
the King* the perfect example of tragic form, and developed his
theory of tragedy from his analysis of it.

Sophocles' fellow citizens respected him sufficiently to vote him into high city office on at least three occasions. He served for a year as chief tribute-collector for Athens' overseas empire. A controversial claim by Aristophanes of Byzantium, in the third century, implies that Sophocles' tribe was so impressed by a production of *Antigone* that they voted him in as one of ten military generals (*strategoi*) in 441–440. Later in life Sophocles was respected as a participant in democratic governance at the highest level. In 411 he was elected to a ten-man commission charged with replacing Athens' discredited democratic governance with an oligarchy, a development that followed the military's catastrophic defeat in Sicily in 413.

Most ancient biographical sources attest to Sophocles' good looks, his easygoing manner, and his enjoyment of life. Athanaeus' multivolume *Deipnosophistai*, a compendium of gossip and dinner chat about and among ancient worthies, includes several vivid passages that reveal Sophocles as both a commanding presence and an impish prankster, ready one moment to put down a schoolmaster's boorish literary criticism and the next to flirt with the wine boy.

Sophocles is also convincingly described as universally respected, with amorous inclinations and intensely religious qualities that, to his contemporaries, did not seem incompatible. Religious piety meant something quite different to an Athenian than the humility, sobriety, and aversion to sensual pleasure it might suggest to us—officially, if not actually. His involvement in various cults, including one dedicated to a god of health and another to the hero Herakles, contributed to his reputation as "loved by the gods" and "the most religious of men." He was celebrated—and worshipped after his death as a hero—for bringing a healing cult (related to Aesculapius and involving a snake) to Athens. It is possible he founded an early version of a hospital. He never flinched from portraying the Greek gods as often wantonly cruel, destroying innocent people, for instance, as punishment for their ancestors' crimes. But the gods in *Antigone*, *Oedipus at Kolonos*, and *Philoktetes* mete out justice with a more even hand.

One remarkable absence in Sophocles' own life was documented suffering of any kind. His luck continued to the moment his body was placed in its tomb. As he lay dying, a Spartan army had once again invaded the Athenian countryside, blocking access to Sophocles' burial site beyond Athens' walls. But after Sophocles' peaceful death the Spartan general allowed the poet's burial party to pass through his lines, apparently out of respect for the god Dionysos.

Robert Bagg

James Scully

NOTE

1. Unless otherwise indicated, the line numbers and note numbers for translations of Sophocles' dramas other than *Oedipus at Kolonos* refer to those in the Harper Perennial *Complete Sophocles* series.

Oedipus at

Kolonos

INTRODUCTION
"HIS DEATH WAS A CAUSE FOR WONDER"

The Oedipus we meet in Kolonos, a lush country village a mile north of Athens, where Sophocles was raised, has suffered through years of blindness, poverty, and exile. He is old and frail, but still recognizable as the fearless, vengeful, and quick-witted hero of *Oedipus the King*. Traits that characterized his youth (and contributed to his downfall) still energize the aged Oedipus as he repeatedly recalls, and forcefully defends, his earlier conduct. Only at the end of his journey, as he approaches the afterlife that Apollo promised would somehow distinguish him, does Oedipus become a gentler and more loving man.

The Greek word for the grace or favor extended by men and gods to the worthy, the needy, the damaged, and the miserable is *charis*. By setting *Oedipus at Kolonos* on the edge of a sacred grove blessed with flowers, grape vines, nightingales, shade trees, and clearings suitable for dancing, Sophocles creates a physical setting where men and gods converge, one that makes manifest the metaphysical space where the human and divine pay their respects and offer *charis* to each other. *Charis* becomes a palpable presence onstage, its promise growing more significant as the drama unfolds.

In the sacred grove of the Eumenides, Oedipus will find the mercy, and in a sense the rebirth, Apollo promised him at Delphi—almost as an afterthought—when as a troubled young man he received the worst news any Greek ever heard from a god: he was doomed to kill his father and his mother would bear his children. Now, within the grove's precincts, the weakened Oedipus will be transformed from a reviled exile into a revered hero. As the classicist John Gould put it, "Nowhere else in Greek tragedy does the primitively mysterious power of boundaries and thresholds, the 'extraterritoriality' of the sacred, make itself felt with the fierce precision that Sophocles achieves" in the song the Old Men sing as they arrive on the scene (1973, 90). We sense immediately the primitive dread aroused by the grove's divine inhabitants. Oedipus, guided by Antigone, hides in the trees as the chorus sweeps angrily onstage. The Old Men denounce the hidden intruder. They scour the grove for signs of him and sing their terror of the all-seeing Furies, whom they refer to circumspectly as the Kindly Ones. To escape the goddesses' withering glances, the old men walk with their eyes lowered. As even the uttering of the Furies' names is forbidden, the prayers they mouth are silent.

Oedipus responds to the Old Men's warnings by emerging from his hiding place in the grove. He gives himself up to them. He won't reenter the grove until a god's voice calls to him in the play's climactic moments. Meanwhile, by dramatizing Oedipus' claims to deserve the gods' *charis*, Sophocles explores a subject that fascinated him—heroes and their deaths as paradigms for the fully empowered human spirit.

Thus the final surviving work by Sophocles, the second of his two dramas about Oedipus, brings his hero's story to a tantalizing but still satisfying conclusion, one we could not have predicted for the broken and abandoned man we saw at the end of *Oedipus the King*. In addition to chronicling Oedipus' reversal of fortune, the *Kolonos* also conveys the wise old citizen-playwright's last reflections on themes keenly important to him: the damage that lives wrecked in one generation inflict on the next; the difference between moral guilt and religious defilement; the responsibilities of parents and children to each other; the miseries of old age; and the greatness of Athens.

The *Kolonos*, which was produced posthumously at the Theater of Dionysos in 401 BCE by Sophocles the Younger, coincides with Athens' darker endgame—the final defeat by Sparta that closed Athens' century-long era of political innovation, military hegemony, and theatrical genius. Sophocles celebrates Athens' past and timeless moral and mythical glory throughout the play—most brilliantly in a song of gratitude to the "mother city, / for the great gifts the gods have given her" (775–776). A few incidents in the plot might also allude to Athens' decline: Polyneikes' reckless and self-obsessed campaign against Thebes recalls Athens' own military failures stretching back to the invasion of Sicily in 415. Theseus' unsentimental appreciation of Oedipus, as well as his swift dispatch of troops that foil Kreon's attempt to abduct Oedipus' daughters, reminds us that skilled and gracious men, like Perikles and Themistokles, once led Athens.

The commanding presence with which Oedipus engages his benefactor Theseus (and his enemies—his own son Polyneikes and his old nemesis Kreon) revives Oedipus' dormant greatness. Cumulative scenes of accusation and defense test and confirm Oedipus' strengths and his sangfroid: his stubbornness, his quick analytic intelligence, his love for his caring daughters, his rhetorical flair, his sense of his own value to others, his unflinching

moral fury. The play's unusual length affords Sophocles the scope
to develop and nuance his vision of an eternally embattled hero.

Modern readers will relate to most of Oedipus' convictions
and obsessions—belief that he's innocent of willful murder and
incest; confidence that he'll achieve the good death the gods
have promised—but will find others puzzling. A look at ancient
Greek religious and social practices will bring these less familiar and ambiguous issues into focus.

We use the word "fate," often casually, to describe the mysterious and invincible (but possibly nonexistent) force that may
or may not govern our lives. Fate, to the Greeks, was a potent
reality. Their word for it is *tyche* (pronounced too-KAY). Both
the English and the Greek words point to life-altering events
that happen outside a person's control. But to possess the ancient context of *tyche*—which may also be translated as "luck"
or "destiny"—we should imagine it as a force that puts constant
pressure on a person's mind, a reality beyond comprehension or
appeal. No wonder then, considering how ordinary Greeks believed *tyche* governed the events of their lives, that plots which
precipitate disaster, as do those of *Oedipus the King* and Euripides' *Medea*, and plots with upbeat outcomes, such as Euripides' *Alkestis* or Aeschylus' *Eumenides*, were equally popular
with Athenian audiences and playwrights. A theatrical plot was
no more likely to be censured for its credulity-straining twists
than a man's action-packed life would have been interpreted
as meaningless happenstance. Both a play's and a life's plot revealed the gods at work and therefore implicitly conveyed to
observers the gods' moral encouragement or their warning.

Just as the concept of the *daimon* helps explain why Oedipus' seemingly rational choices turn out so badly in *Oedipus the King*, the *charis* finally granted him by the gods illuminates the significance of Oedipus' death in the *Kolonos*. *Oedipus the King* shows the gods—through their proxy, the personal *daimon* who acts on behalf of Apollo to govern the events of Oedipus' life—using cruel duplicity to destroy him. The *Kolonos*, on the other hand, reveals the gods' change of heart, their ultimate, if long withheld, concern and grace. Both dramas thus share the goal of understanding and radically reinterpreting past events in the hero's life that were predicted and, apparently, ordained by the gods. The earlier Oedipus' intellect was helpless against the malevolence of his *daimon*. But in the *Kolonos*, Oedipus' justifications, conscious choices, and cogent analyses are reinterpreted, rewarded, and finally blessed.

The secondary prophecy Apollo made to the young Oedipus— that at the point of death, safe haven would await him in a grove of the Eumenides near Athens—parallels the transformation in Aeschylus' *Orestia* in which Orestes' Furies, once the hounding tormentors of all kin murderers, are transformed by the gods at Orestes' trial in Athens into benign protectors of the family. Both Oedipus and Orestes live through crises wherein their traumatic actions change who they are for the better. Fury has driven Oedipus to commit the acts that fulfilled Apollo's original prophecy. His once self-destructive fury now attacks only his outward enemies—and will enduringly protect what Oedipus now values, his adopted city Athens. He achieves an inner peacefulness during his final hour that precedes his entry into Hades and his promised emergence into the afterlife as a hero.

Oedipus' sexual violation of his mother and the killing of his father are both forgiven and perhaps evoked during the miraculous

vanishing into the Earth that Sophocles lets us imagine through
the Messenger, a witness who does not have a close-up view—only
Theseus has that privilege—but who tries to imagine what he par-
tially sees. Here the Messenger recounts the death of Oedipus:

> But the exact nature
> of the death Oedipus died, no man
> but Theseus could tell you. Zeus didn't
> incinerate him with a lightning blast,
> no sudden squall blew inland from the sea.
> So it was either a god spiriting
> him away, or else the Earth's lower world—
> her deep foundations—opening to him,
> for he felt nothing but welcoming kindness.
>
> When this man vanished, there was no sorrow.
> He suffered no sickness. His death, like no
> other man's, was a cause for wonder.   (1812–1823)

The Messenger takes it upon himself to note what Oedipus' death was not—no sudden skyward abduction by Zeus, no
lightning blast, no hurricane blowing him out to sea. Sorrow,
suffering, sickness—none is present. It was indeed a death that
suggested forgiveness, a death administered in all its gentleness
by the Earth Mother, Gaia. She opened to him, with no sugges-
tion of violation, "for he felt nothing but welcoming kindness"
(1820). After all the horrific violations he committed unaware,
such a death was indeed "a cause for wonder."

Oedipus at Kolonos

The play opens in the countryside a mile and a quarter northwest of the Acropolis in Athens. A sacred grove is at stage rear. Olives, grape vines, crocus, and narcissus bloom within it; birds sing and fountains splash. A path leads over the gentle rise down into the grove's depths. A natural stone bench sits upstage just inside the grove. A rock ledge running across the slope has a flat sitting place at its lower downstage end; near it is a statue of the hero Kolonos. Entering from the road to Thebes, on the spectators' left,

ANTIGONE guides her father, the aged OEDIPUS, onstage. Both are dusty and weary. OEDIPUS carries a staff and a traveler's pouch.

OEDIPUS

Daughter, I'm old and blind. Where are we now,
Antigone? Have we come to a town?
(calling out)
Who will indulge Wandering Oedipus
today—with some food and a place to sleep?

I ask little, I'm given less, but it's
enough. The blows I've suffered
have taught me acquiescence. So has Time,
my enduring companion.
So has my noble birth.

Daughter, if you see somewhere   10
to rest—on public land, or in a grove
set aside for the gods—
guide me to it, sit me down there.
Then we'll determine where we are.
We're strangers here. We must listen
to the locals and do what they say.

ANTIGONE

My poor exhausted father!
Oedipus, the towers guarding the city
seem far off. I have the feeling
we're in some holy place—   20

there's so much olive and laurel and grape vine
running wild. Listen. Deep inside, it's packed
with nightingales! Rest on this ledge.
For an old man, this has been a long trek.

OEDIPUS

Ease the blind man down. Be my lookout.

ANTIGONE

No need to tell me! I've been doing this awhile.

OEDIPUS sits on a stone outcrop just inside the grove.

OEDIPUS

Now, can you tell me where we are?

ANTIGONE

Athens, but I don't know which part.

OEDIPUS

Travelers on the road told us that much.

ANTIGONE

Shouldn't I go ask what this place is called?   30

OEDIPUS

Do that, child. If this place can support life.

ANTIGONE

But people *do* live here. No need to search.
I see a man nearby. Right over there.

OEDIPUS

Is he headed in our direction?

Enter STRANGER, who strides toward them.

ANTIGONE

(whispering)
No. He's already close. Whatever seems
called for, say it to him now. He's here.

OEDIPUS

Stranger, this girl—whose eyes see for us both—
tells me that you've arrived opportunely,
to help us resolve our quandary . . .

STRANGER

                                    Hold it.
Before you start asking *me* questions,   40
get off that rock! You're on forbidden ground.

ANTIGONE helps OEDIPUS rise slowly to his feet.

OEDIPUS

What kind of ground? Belonging to which gods?

STRANGER

It's off-limits. No one's allowed to live here.
It's sacred to some fearsome goddesses—
daughters of Darkness and the Earth.

OEDIPUS

By what respectful name do you call them—
since I'm about to offer them a prayer?

STRANGER

People here call them the Kindly Ones—
the goddesses who see everything.
Other places might give them harsher names.   50

OEDIPUS

Then let them be kind to *this* suppliant!
I'll never leave this sacred ground.

STRANGER

Why do you say that?

OEDIPUS

It all fits: *here* is where I meet my fate.

STRANGER

Well, then, I won't presume to drive you out.
Not till I get permission from the city.

STRANGER starts to leave.

OEDIPUS

For god's sake, man! Don't scorn me because I
look like a tramp. I need to know something.

STRANGER

Then say what you need. I won't hold back.

OEDIPUS

This place we've entered—what do they call it?   60

STRANGER

I'll say only what I know *personally*.
This entire grove is holy and belongs
to grim Poseidon. Prometheus the firegod
also has a shrine here. That rock ledge
you're on is our country's brass-footed threshold.
It anchors Athens. The horseman over there—

—*STRANGER gestures toward an equestrian statue*—

is Kolonos, who settled the farmland
hereabouts. We've all taken his name. That's
the story, stranger. Kolonos isn't
so much a legend as a presence we feel.   70

OEDIPUS

Then people do live around here?

STRANGER

Of course! They're named after that hero there.

STRANGER nods toward the statue of Kolonos.

OEDIPUS

You have a king? Or do the people rule?

STRANGER

We have a king who governs from Athens.

OEDIPUS

Whose eloquence and strength brought him to power?

STRANGER

Theseus. Old King Aigeus' son.

OEDIPUS

I wonder . . . could someone from here go find him?

STRANGER

To take a message? Bring him back? What for?

OEDIPUS

So he may be hugely repaid for a small kindness.

STRANGER

Tell me, how can a blind man be of use?   80

OEDIPUS

My words, every one of them, can see.

STRANGER

Look, friend, don't do anything reckless.
Your bearing tells me you're from noble stock,
but it's clear you're down on your luck.
Stay put, right where I found you, while I go
let the men in town know what's happened.
Never mind Athens—*we* will decide
whether you stay here or move on.

Exit STRANGER.

OEDIPUS

Has the stranger left, child?

ANTIGONE

He's gone, Father. You can speak freely.   90
It's quiet now. I'm the only one here.

OEDIPUS *assumes a posture of prayer.*

OEDIPUS

Ladies whose eyes we dread, since your grove
is the first in this land where I've come to pray,
don't be unkind
either to me or to Apollo.
When the god condemned me to such grief,
he assured me my long life would end here—
that I'd find a haven, and be taken in
by vengeful goddesses, to be a source

of strength to those who welcomed me, and a curse   100
to those who drove me out. The god promised
he'd show a sign—an earthquake, some thunder,
or lightning flamed from Zeus' own hand.

It must have been, Ladies, a trustworthy
omen from you that led me to this place.
Why else would you be the first deities
I've met on my travels? I—a sober man—
find my way to you, who spurn wine. What else
could have brought me to this rough stone bench?

Please, Goddesses, do as Apollo bids: 110
grant me a clear path to my life's end—unless
I seem in some way beneath your concern,
profaned as I am by the worst evils
a man may endure. Respond to me,
delightful daughters of primeval darkness!
And help me Athens, most
honored city in Greece,
homeland of Pallas Athena! Pity
this feeble ghost of the man Oedipus.
My body hasn't always looked like this.   120

ANTIGONE

Shhh, be quiet now. Some old men—they look
ancient!—have come searching for you.

OEDIPUS

I'll be quiet. Get me to the trees,
off the road, so I can hear what they say.
What we learn will help us
decide our best course of action.

ANTIGONE guides OEDIPUS up the slope and into the grove. Chorus of OLD
MEN enters. Gracefully, they probe along the grove's edge in a coordinated
dancing movement while singing their entry song.

OLD MEN

Look for him,
though we don't know
who he is, or where
he's hiding now.   130
He's bolted for cover,
totally brazen!
Search the whole grove.
Look sharp, look everywhere.
The old fellow's
a foreigner, an intruder.
No native would invade
prohibited grounds
of virgins so violent,
so uncontrollable—   140
their very names
we fear to say out loud.
We walk in their midst,
eyes lowered, not breathing

a word, though our lips
mouth silent prayers.

LEADER

We've heard the report:
Someone with no respect
for the goddesses has arrived.
But looking across the sacred glen   150
I don't see him or his hiding place.

OEDIPUS steps forward from the foliage.

OEDIPUS

I'm here. The man you're looking for. I see
with my ears, as people say of the blind.

LEADER

Aggghh! Aggghh!
The sight of you, the sound of your voice, appalls us.

OEDIPUS

Don't look at me as though I'm some outlaw.

LEADER

Spare us, Zeus! Who is this haughty old man?

OEDIPUS

Not someone whose life you might envy—
you men charged with guarding your country!

Isn't that obvious? Why else   160
would I walk as I do, dependent
on other people's eyes, and tethered,
large as I am, to this frail creature?

LEADER
Ah! Then you were born blind?
You must have led a long,
bleak life. Take our advice:
Don't add one more curse
to your miseries. You've gone
too far! Please step back!
Don't go stumbling   170
through that green glade
where speech is forbidden,
where we pour
clear water from a bowl,
blending it
with honey-sweet libations.

Watch yourself,
stranger with such
horrendous luck—
stand back, walk away!   180
Move further back!
Do you hear me? If you
have something to tell us,
get off that sacred ground!
Speak only

where talk is allowed.
Until then, keep quiet.

OEDIPUS

Daughter, what should we do?

ANTIGONE

(conferring quietly with OEDIPUS)
Respect their customs, Father.
Do as they ask. Be deferential.   190

OEDIPUS

Give me your hand, then.

ANTIGONE

                          Here, feel mine.

OEDIPUS, with ANTIGONE supporting him, very cautiously approaches the
OLD MEN.

OEDIPUS

I'm going to trust you, strangers. Don't
betray me when I leave this holy ground.

LEADER

Nobody will force you to leave
this resting place against your will.

OEDIPUS pauses in his progress.

OEDIPUS

Further?

LEADER

Keep going.

OEDIPUS

More?

LEADER

Keep him moving, girl, you can see the path.

ANTIGONE

Come on, Father.   200
Keep stepping
into the dark
as I lead you.

LEADER

You are, old man, a stranger
in a strange land.
Accustom yourself
to hating what our city
despises and revering
what it loves.

OEDIPUS

Guide me, child, to some spot   210
where I can speak and listen

without offending the gods.
Let's not fight the inevitable.

LEADER

Stop right there. Don't move
beyond that rock ledge.

OEDIPUS

Stop here?

LEADER

That's far enough, I'm telling you!

OEDIPUS

May I sit down?

LEADER

Yes. Edge sideways and squat down on that rock.

ANTIGONE holds OEDIPUS and guides his steps.

ANTIGONE

Father, let me do this. Take one   220
easy step after another . . .

OEDIPUS

                    Oh, my.

ANTIGONE

. . . leaning your tired body
on my loving arm.

OEDIPUS

I'm sorry for my weakness.

ANTIGONE sits him on the rock ledge downstage.

LEADER

Poor fellow, now that you're at ease,
tell us who you are in the world.
Who would want to be moved about
in such excruciating pain?
Tell us where you live.

OEDIPUS

Strangers, I have no home! But please don't . . .   230

LEADER

What don't you want us to ask, old man?

OEDIPUS

Don't! Just don't ask who I am.
No questions, no more probing.

LEADER

Is there a reason?

OEDIPUS

The horror I was born to.

LEADER

Go on.

OEDIPUS

(whispering)

Child, what should I tell them?

LEADER

Speak up, stranger: tell us
your bloodlines. Start with your father.

OEDIPUS

What's going to happen to me, child?

ANTIGONE

You've been pushed to the brink. Better tell them.

OEDIPUS

All right, I'll say it. There's no way to hide it.   240

LEADER

You both take too much time. Go on, speak.

OEDIPUS

You've heard of Laios' son . . .

OLD MEN

Aaaaah!

OEDIPUS

. . . and the house of Labdakos . . .

OLD MEN

O Zeus!

OEDIPUS

     . . . and doomed Oedipus?

LEADER

That's who you are?

OEDIPUS

Don't fear my words . . .

OLD MEN

Aaagghhh! Aaagghhh!

As their cries of apprehension overwhelm OEDIPUS' *previous words, the* OLD MEN *en bloc turn away from him.*

OEDIPUS

     . . . because I am a broken man.

OLD MEN

Aaagghhh! Aaagghhh!

OEDIPUS

What's going to happen, child?

LEADER

Get out of here! Leave our country!   250

OEDIPUS

And the promise you made me?
How do you plan to honor that?

LEADER

When someone who's been wronged
defends himself by striking back,
Fate doesn't punish him. And when
deception is used to counter
deceit, it should cause pain, not gratitude.
Stand up! Now! Get off that seat! Leave this land
as fast as you can walk, so you won't burden
our city with your deadly contagion.   260

ANTIGONE

Strangers, so full of holy sentiments!
You can't abide my agèd father's presence,
can you? Because you've heard the rumors
about those actions he took in ignorance.
Think how unhappy it makes me
to plead with you on my father's behalf.
Strangers, I am looking at you with eyes
that aren't blind, and I beg *you* to see *me*

as though I were your family—and to feel
responsible for this afflicted person.   270
Our miserable lives depend on you
as if you all were gods. Give us the help
that we've stopped hoping for!

I'm begging you, in the name
of whatever you hold dear—
whether it's your child or your wife,
your fortune or your god!
                    However hard
you look, you'll never find a man who can
escape his own fate-driven actions.

LEADER

We pity both of you, daughter—   280
you and your father, Oedipus.
You've led unfortunate lives.
But we fear the gods, we fear their anger,
if we say more than we've already said.

OEDIPUS

What good are fame and glory, if they just
trickle away and accomplish nothing?
Men call Athens the most god-fearing city,
a safe haven for persecuted strangers,
their best hope when they need a helping hand.
But how do these virtues benefit me   290
when you force me to climb down these ledges

and depart from your country? Does my *name*
frighten you? My appearance? Or my past deeds?
I performed every one of those actions,
you should know, but I willed none. You want me
to speak of my relations with my father
and mother—is that the source of your fear?

I have no doubt it is exactly that.
Yet, tell me: how is my *nature* evil—
if all I did was to return a blow?   300
How could I have been guilty, even if
I'd known where my actions would take me
while I was living them? But those who tried
to murder me—*they knew* what they were doing.

My friends, the gods inspired you to drive
me off that ledge. So respect these same gods—
and grant me the refuge that you've offered.
Don't act *now* as though gods don't exist.
They protect those who fear them,
but they also destroy those who don't.   310
And no godless mortal ever escapes.

Let the gods show you the way: don't blacken
Athens' reputation by taking part
in crimes of irreverence! I am
a suppliant to whom you promised
safety. Don't break that promise. And don't
shun me because of my disfigured face.

I've come here a devout and sacred man,
and I'll prove myself useful to your people.
When the man who holds power arrives,   320
whoever that may be, I will tell him
everything. Until then, do me no harm.

LEADER

We're impressed by the way you think, old man.
How could we not be? You speak with force.
We don't take you lightly, but we'd prefer
to have our rulers deal with this problem.

OEDIPUS

Where then, my friends, is this leader of yours?

LEADER

He's now in Athens, his home city. The same
person who sent us went on to find him.

OEDIPUS

Do you think he'll have sufficient   330
concern and regard for a blind old man
to travel all the way out here himself?

LEADER

He will come as soon as he hears your name.

OEDIPUS

And how will he hear my name?

LEADER

                      It's a long road,
but it's busy with foot traffic. News spreads
quickly. Don't worry. He'll recognize your name,
then come immediately to this place.
Your story's widely known, old man. Even
if he's asleep and wakes slowly,
word you're here will bring him in a hurry.   340

OEDIPUS

His coming will help Athens, and help me.
A good man is always his own best friend.

ANTIGONE looks offstage, brightens, and then calls out loudly.

ANTIGONE

O Zeus! What do I say now, Father? Or even think?

OEDIPUS

What do you see, Antigone?

ANTIGONE

(raising her voice)

                      A woman riding
a young Sicilian horse. Wearing a hat
from Thessaly to keep sun off her face.
What can I say? Is she, or isn't she?
Am I hallucinating? Yes? No?
I can't tell yet. Yes! YES!

There's no one else it could be.   350
As she comes closer, I can see her
smiling at me. It's my sister, Ismene!

OEDIPUS

What's that you're shouting, girl?

ANTIGONE

(still shouting)

That I see your daughter and my sister!
You'll recognize her as soon as she speaks.

*Enter ISMENE, having just dismounted from a small horse. She is
accompanied by her Servant.*

ISMENE

Father! Sister! It's wonderful to say those names!
It was so hard to find you. Now that I have,
I can hardly see you through my tears.

OEDIPUS

You've come, child?

ISMENE

                    I hate to see you like this, Father.

OEDIPUS

But you've joined us.

ISMENE

Not without some trouble.   360

OEDIPUS

Touch me, daughter.

ISMENE

Each of you take a hand.

OEDIPUS, ANTIGONE, and ISMENE join hands and hold them a while.

OEDIPUS

My daughters. Sisters.

ISMENE

Two wretched lives!

OEDIPUS

Hers and mine?

ISMENE

Yes. And my life as well.

OEDIPUS

Why did you come, child?

ISMENE

I care about you, Father.

OEDIPUS

Then you missed me?

ISMENE

I did. And I bring news
I wanted you to hear from me.
I also brought our last faithful servant.

OEDIPUS

Our family's menfolk, your brothers—
where are they when we need them?

ISMENE

They are . . . wherever they are. Grim times for them.   370

OEDIPUS

Those two boys imitate the Egyptians
in how they think and how they run their lives.
Egyptian men stay in their houses weaving,
while their women are out earning a living.
Your brothers, who should be here helping me,
are back home keeping house like little girls,
while you two shoulder your father's hardships.
Antigone has been traveling with me
since she outgrew the care a child needs.
She gained enough strength to be an old man's   380
guide, picking her way barefoot through forests,
hungry, rain-drenched, sun-scorched.
                                        Home comforts

took second place to caring for her father.
And you, Ismene, slipped out of Thebes
undetected so many times—to bring
the latest oracles to your father.
You were my eyes inside Thebes after I
was banished. Ismene, what's the news
you've brought? Why have you come?
I'm sure you haven't traveled here empty-   390
handed. Is there something I should fear?

ISMENE

Father, I'd rather not describe
the trouble I had trying to find you.
Just let it be! Retelling it
would only revive all the misery.

It's the real trouble your miserable sons are in—
it's their wrath I've come to tell you about.
They were keen, at first, to let Kreon rule,
so as not to pollute the city, well
aware the curse we inherit from way back   400
still holds your house in a death grip.
But spurred on by a god, and by their own
disturbed minds, my brothers—three times cursed!—
began battling each other for dominance
and the king's throne in Thebes.

                              Now that hothead,
Eteokles, your youngest, has stripped
Polyneikes, your firstborn, of all power

and driven him out of the country.
Polyneikes was, from the reports I hear,
exiled to Argos. There he married power,   410
gaining friends willing to fight his battles—
determined to make Argos glorious
if it can conquer Thebes,
or to lift Thebes' reputation
sky-high should Argos lose.
It isn't just loose talk, father,
it has become horrible fact.
When will the gods lighten
your troubles? I wish I knew.

OEDIPUS

Do you hold out some hope that the gods   420
might take notice and end my suffering?

ISMENE

I do, Father. I have new oracles.

OEDIPUS

What are they? What do they say, daughter?

ISMENE

That your own people will someday need you,
living—and dead—to ensure their survival.

OEDIPUS

How could a man like me save anyone?

ISMENE

They say: you will hold Thebes' life in your hands.

OEDIPUS

When I'm nothing . . . how can I still be a man?

ISMENE

The gods who ruined you will now restore you.

OEDIPUS

Does little good to restore an old man   430
after they have laid waste to his youth.

ISMENE

Listen! The gods *will* transform you, and Kreon
will come here earlier than you might think.

OEDIPUS

Has he a plan, child? Tell me.

ISMENE

To station you at the Theban frontier,
but prevent you from crossing over.

OEDIPUS

What help am I if I'm outside their borders?

ISMENE

It's your tomb. If it's not paid proper respect,
that could cause them serious trouble.

OEDIPUS

They shouldn't need a god to tell them that.   440

ISMENE

It's still the reason they want you nearby,
not off someplace where you'd be in charge.

OEDIPUS

Then will they bury me in Theban earth?

ISMENE

Father, that's not allowed. You killed your father.

OEDIPUS

Then they must never have me in their power!

ISMENE

If they don't, things will go badly for Thebes.

OEDIPUS

What will cause things to go badly, daughter?

ISMENE

Your rage, when they're deployed around your tomb.

OEDIPUS

Who told you, child, what you have just told me?

ISMENE

Sacred envoys sent to the Delphic hearth.   450

OEDIPUS

Did the god truly say this about me?

ISMENE

All the returning envoys swore he did.

OEDIPUS

Did either of my sons hear them say it?

ISMENE

They heard it and they both knew what it meant.

OEDIPUS

With this knowledge, did those scoundrels
put the kingship ahead of helping me?

ISMENE

It hurts me to say this, Father. Yes, they did.

OEDIPUS

Gods, don't interfere with this brawl you've ordained!
But give me the right to decide how it ends—
this battle toward which my sons lift up spears   460
and on which they're now dead set. May my son
in power, who wields the scepter, lose it.
May my exiled son never make it home.
When I was driven shamefully from Thebes,
they made no move to stop it or help me.
They were spectators to my banishment.
They heard me proclaimed a homeless outcast!

You might think that Thebes acted properly,
that it gave me what I once craved. That's wrong.
On the far-off day when my fury seethed,   470
a death by stoning was my heartfelt wish.
But there was no one willing to grant it.
Later, when my suffering diminished,
I realized my rage had gone too far
in punishing my mistakes. Only then
did the city decide to force me out—
after all those years. And my own two sons,
who could have saved their father, did nothing.
It would have taken just one word. But I
wandered off into permanent exile.   480
My two unmarried girls fed me as best
they could. They sheltered and protected me,
my only family. But my sons traded
their father for power and a kingdom.

You can be certain I'll give them no help
in fighting their battles, and they will gain
nothing from having been rulers of Thebes.
I know that because, when I heard the oracles
this girl brought, I recalled some prophecies—
ones Phoibos Apollo has now fulfilled.   490

I'm ready. Let them send Kreon to find me—
or anyone who's powerful in Thebes.
If you strangers, together with those
intimidating goddesses who live

among you, are willing to enlist me,
you'll get a champion in the bargain,
someone who will defend your country
against its enemies, and damage his own.

LEADER

You've earned our pity, Oedipus,
both you and your daughters here.   500
And because you've offered to defend us,
I'm going to give you some advice.

OEDIPUS

Whatever my host wants done, I'll do.

LEADER

Ask atonement from the goddesses you first
met here, and whose ground you've invaded.

OEDIPUS

By what means? Tell me what I must do, friends.

LEADER

Dip water from a stream that flows year round,
wash your hands in it, then bring some here.

OEDIPUS

And when I've brought this pure water, what then?

LEADER

You'll find bowls made by a skilled craftsman.   510
Adorn their handles and their rims.

OEDIPUS

With branches or wool cloths—and then what?

LEADER

Gather fresh-cut fleece from a she-lamb.

OEDIPUS

How shall I end the ritual?

LEADER

Face the sunrise and pour an offering.

OEDIPUS

From the bowls you've just described?

LEADER

Spill some from each bowl, then empty the last.

OEDIPUS

Tell me what to put in the bowls.

LEADER

No wine. Just pure water sweetened with honey.

OEDIPUS

After I've drenched the ground under the trees?   520

LEADER

Using both hands, set out three bundles of nine
olive twigs each, while you recite a prayer.

OEDIPUS

That's it—get to the heart of the matter.

LEADER

Pray that the goddesses called the Gracious Ones
protect the suppliant, in their kindness,
and grant him a safe refuge. That's your prayer,
or someone else's who will pray for you.
Don't raise your voice, pray quietly,
and, without looking back, leave.
Do as I've said, and I'm sure you'll succeed.   530
If you don't, stranger, I'm afraid for you.

OEDIPUS

Daughters, have you heard what our friend here said?

ANTIGONE

We heard. What would you like us to do?

OEDIPUS

I lack the eyes—and the strength—to go myself.
My double loss. One of you must do it.

It is possible for one living soul
to pay a debt that's owed by ten thousand,
provided it's done with conviction.
One of you go—but don't leave me alone.
My body's too weak to move without help.   540

ISMENE

I'll carry out the ritual, but someone
must show me the right place to perform it.

LEADER

Go around to the far side of the grove.
If you need anything else, there's a man
living nearby who will point you the way.

ISMENE

I'll go now, Sister. You stay with Father.
Helping a parent who can't help himself
should never seem a burden.

Exit ISMENE and her Servant.

LEADER

Unpleasant it may be, stranger, to stir up
a long dormant grief. Yet there is something   550
I would like to hear straight from you.

OEDIPUS

                              What's your concern?

LEADER

That bitter, incurable anguish—
the kind you had to wrestle with.

OEDIPUS

Out of consideration for a guest,
don't dwell on my unfortunate past.

LEADER

Your story's widely told, my friend.
I'd like to hear the truth of it.

OEDIPUS

(pronouncing with a brusque hissing sound)
Ssstop!

LEADER

Hear me out, let me speak!

OEDIPUS

(aspirated vowel; spoken querulously)
Whhhy?   560

LEADER

You owe me this. I've granted all you've asked.

OEDIPUS

I suffered anguish, friends,
suffered what my own

blind actions caused.
But let the gods testify:
I chose to do none.

LEADER

Then how did this happen?

OEDIPUS

Thebes married me, who suspected nothing,
to a woman who would destroy me.

LEADER

Was she your mother, as I've heard,   570
who shared your infamous marriage bed?

OEDIPUS

She was. Your words feel
harsh as death in my ears.
And those daughters I fathered . . .

LEADER

What are you saying now?

OEDIPUS

                    —twin scourges—

LEADER

O Zeus!

OEDIPUS

... were born from the birth pangs
of the mother we shared.

LEADER

They're your daughters, and ...

OEDIPUS

Yes! They're my sisters.

OLD MEN

(low whispering)
How horrible.

OEDIPUS

Oh yes! A thousand evils   580
surge back, all through me.

LEADER

Then you suffered ...

OEDIPUS

I suffered an indelible torment.

LEADER

Then you've sinned ...

OEDIPUS

There was no sin.

LEADER

How did you not?

OEDIPUS

I was presented with a gift—
one that would break my heart—
to repay me for all the help
I gave Thebes. It was a gift
I should never have accepted.   590

LEADER

Horrible. And then? You killed . . . ?

OEDIPUS

Why this? What are you asking me?

LEADER

                                        . . . your father?

OEDIPUS

You open one old wound after another.

LEADER

Then you killed him.

OEDIPUS

                        Yes, I killed him. But I have . . .

LEADER

You have what?

OEDIPUS

      Justice on my side.

LEADER

                     How could that be?

OEDIPUS

Let me tell you. The men
I fought and killed
would have killed me.
Before the law
my hands are clean.   600
My actions were driven
not by malice,
but by ignorance.

One of Theseus' Men enters, whispers to the LEADER, and then exits.

LEADER

Aigeus' son, our king, has arrived, willing
to do all you have asked of him.

Enter THESEUS, who walks up and examines OEDIPUS.

THESEUS

For years I've heard that you had done
bloody damage to your eyes—so I
recognize you, son of Laios. What I learned
on my way here made me almost certain.
And to see you now at your journey's end   610

removes all doubt. Your clothes, your ravaged face,
tell me your name. Oedipus, I
truly pity you. And I will help you.
You and this poor girl have come here
suddenly—why? To request a favor
from Athens and from me? If so, ask it.
You would need to tell me an appalling
story indeed before I'd turn you down.
Remember, I was also raised in exile,
combating threats to my life of a kind   620
no other man has ever had to face.
I would never refuse a homeless man—
which you are—my help. I'm also mortal,
like you, with no greater assurance
than you have that I'll be alive tomorrow.

OEDIPUS

There's little I need add, Theseus.
With a few gracious words
you've said exactly who I am, and who
my father was, and what country I'm from—
so nothing remains. Except to tell you   630
what most concerns me. Then I'll be silent.

THESEUS

Go on. Say what you mean. I must know.

OEDIPUS

I came to offer you my disfigured
body as a gift. Though not pleasant

to look at, it will generate benefits
beauty could not.

THESEUS

                This advantage
you claim to have brought us—what is it?

OEDIPUS

In time you will know. But not for a while.

THESEUS

Your . . . enhancement—when will it be revealed?

OEDIPUS

After I'm dead and you have buried me.   640

THESEUS

You ask me to oversee your last rites,
but say nothing of your life before then.

OEDIPUS

Grant my wish. Everything else will follow.

THESEUS

This favor you're asking seems a small one.

OEDIPUS

Take care. This is no trivial matter.

THESEUS

Then you anticipate trouble. From your sons?

OEDIPUS

King, my sons want to return me to Thebes.

THESEUS

If that's your desire, why would you refuse?

OEDIPUS

(loudly and with fury)

Because, when I wished to stay, *they* refused!

THESEUS

Fool! When you're in trouble, rage never helps.   650

OEDIPUS

Wait till you've heard me out. Then chastise me.

THESEUS

Go on. I shouldn't speak without the facts.

OEDIPUS

Theseus, I have suffered terribly.

THESEUS

You mean the ancient curse on your family.

OEDIPUS

No. Not that story every Greek has heard.

THESEUS

Then what superhuman pain *do* you suffer?

OEDIPUS

Here's what my two sons did to me.
They banished me from my homeland. I can't
return because I killed my own father.

THESEUS

If that's the case, why would Thebes want you back?   660

OEDIPUS

God's voice will *compel* them to take me back.

THESEUS

Oracles must have frightened them. Of what?

OEDIPUS

That Fate will strike them down in your country.

THESEUS

And what could cause such hatred between us?

OEDIPUS

Gentle son of Aigeus, only the gods
never grow old and die. All-powerful
Time ravages the rest. Just as the Earth
decays, so does the body's strength. When trust
between people dies, betrayal begins.
A spirit of respect can never last   670

between two friends, or between two cities,
because sooner or later resentment
kills all friendships. Though sometimes they revive.

The weather now is sunny between Thebes
and Athens, but Time in due course will bring
on a war sparked by a minor grievance—
endless days and nights in which Theban spears
shatter the peace they had promised to keep.

Then my dead body, slumbering, buried,
deathly cold, will drink their hot blood—if Zeus   680
is still Zeus, if Apollo spoke the truth.
But since there's no pleasure in pronouncing
words that should never be said, I will stop.
Keep *your* word and you'll never be sorry
you welcomed Oedipus to your city—unless
the gods abort their promises to me.

LEADER

From the beginning, King, this man has shown
he has the nerve to keep every promise
he's made to our country—and he'll keep more.

THESEUS

Who would refuse the kindness of a man   690
like this? We welcome him to our home fires.
As our wartime ally he's earned the right.
Now he comes asking our gods to help him,

an act with no small implication
for Athens and myself. I value
what he brings. Reject his offers?
Never! I'll settle him in our land
with the rights of a citizen.
If it's the stranger's desire to live *here,*
(turning toward the LEADER)
I will charge *you* with his protection.   700
Or he may wish to join me.
                              Oedipus,
it's your decision. I'll respect your choice.

OEDIPUS

O Zeus, do your utmost for this man.

THESEUS

What is your pleasure? To live in my house?

OEDIPUS

If that were allowed. But *here* is the place . . .

THESEUS

Here? What will you do here? I'm not opposed . . .

OEDIPUS

. . . where I will punish those who drove me out.

THESEUS

Then the great gift you meant—is your presence?

OEDIPUS

Yes. If you keep the pledges you gave me.

THESEUS

Don't doubt me. I will never betray you.   710

OEDIPUS

I won't demand an oath from you—as though
you were a man who couldn't be trusted.

THESEUS

But that's all I can offer you: my word.

OEDIPUS

How then will you act . . .

THESEUS

                    What is your worst fear?

OEDIPUS

That troops will come.

THESEUS

                    My men will deal with them.

OEDIPUS

Take care that when you leave me . . .

THESEUS

Please. Don't tell me what to do.

OEDIPUS

How can I *not* be afraid?

THESEUS

                My heart isn't pounding.

OEDIPUS

You don't know what they threaten . . .

THESEUS

                    I know this:
no men will seize you unless I allow it.   720
And if they brag how simple it will be
to kidnap you, I think the sea they're crossing
will prove too vast and too rough for their skills.
For now, take courage. Aside from any
assurance *I've* given, it was *Apollo*
who sent you. While I'm gone,
my word will protect you.

Exit THESEUS.

OLD MEN

You've come, stranger, to shining Kolonos
abounding with horses
and Earth's loveliest farms.   730
Here the Nightingale
sings her long clear trills
under green forest trees
laden with apples and berries.

In the wine-dark ivy she sings,
in the forbidden
thickets of goddesses
untroubled by hot sun
or the chill blast of winter.

She sings in the clearings   740
where Dionysos dances
among the everloving
maenads who raised him.
Here, drinking dew from the sky
morning after morning,
narcissi flourish.
Their heavenly blossoms
crown two immortals,
Persephone and Demeter—sunlight
illumines the golden crocus.   750

Bountiful fountains send Kephisos
cascading down the mountain.
He never stops flowing, greening
all that grows, pouring daily
his pure waters
through the valley's nurturing hills.
Nor do the Muses,
singing in harmony, or the Goddess of Love
with golden reins in her hands,
stay away long.   760

A tree not found in Asia,
or on the Dorian Island of Pelops,
lives here, a tree born from itself,
a tree no one plants.
A terror to enemy spears,
the gray-green olive
grows freely on our land,
nourishing our children.
Neither the young men nor the old
will shatter and destroy it,   770
for Zeus of the Olive Groves,
and Athena with seagreen eyes,
guard it with tireless glare.

And now with all our strength we sing
our gratitude to our mother city,
for the great gifts the gods have given her:
that peerless glory of our land,
the strength of stallions, the speed of colts—
and the rolling power of the sea.
It was you, son of Kronos,   780
who gave Kolonos our throne,
and you, Lord Poseidon,
who taught us to harness, out on these roads,
the fury of horses, taught us to drive
the long-limbed oar that pulses us
over salt seas, in pursuit
of fifty Nereids' skittering feet.

ANTIGONE's attention is drawn offstage left.

ANTIGONE

You've praised your land beyond all others—
prove now you can act on those glowing words.

OEDIPUS

What makes you say that to them, daughter?   790

ANTIGONE

Kreon's arriving, Father, backed by troops.

OEDIPUS

Can I trust these kind old men to protect me?

LEADER

Don't worry, you're in good hands. I may have aged,
but this country has lost none of its strength.

Enter KREON, escorted by his armed Soldiers.

KREON

You men must be the local nobility.
I detect some fear showing in your eyes
at my arrival. Don't be alarmed.
There's no need for hostile murmuring.
I haven't come intending to use force.
I'm an old man. Yours is a powerful city,   800
if ever there was one in Greece. So yes—

I was sent here, on account of my age,
to reason with that man, and bring him home.
No single person sent me—all Thebes did.
Kinship demands I show greater concern
for his troubles than do my countrymen.
(turning to face OEDIPUS)
You've suffered for too long, Oedipus.
Please hear me out, then we can both go home.
It's high time your fellow Kadmeans
took you back. More than anyone else, I   810
share your sorrows, old man, now that I see
how you live in your miserable exile—
drifting in constant want, with only this girl
as your servant.

           I never thought her life
would sink to such gross squalor, but it has:
tending to you, to your personal needs,
living in poverty. And at her age,
with no experience of men, she's ripe
for the first vulgar lout who comes along.
Those are harsh judgments, aren't they, alas,   820
on you and on me? On our whole family.

Since there's no way to hide your obvious
degradation, Oedipus, please agree
to placate our family gods by coming
home to the house and city of your fathers.
Thank Athens for her kindness as you leave,
for she deserves it. But your birthplace must,

if you would do the right thing, have the final
claim on you. Long ago, she nurtured you.

OEDIPUS

You! You'll try anything! You have based your   830
insidious arguments on the most
ethical grounds. But why make the attempt?
Why try to slide a noose around my neck?
That would cause me unendurable pain.

Some time ago, when I was tormented
by self-inflicted agony and wanted
with all my heart to be banished from Thebes,
you refused me. Later, when my grief eased
and I wished to remain home, you drove me
from my house, off the land, into exile,   840
without one thought of this kinship you claim.

Now this time, seeing the friendly welcome
Athens and her people have given me,
you try to abduct me—your harsh purpose
sheathed in amiable words. What joy is there
in kindness that's imposed against our will?
Suppose someone refuses to help you—
though you've begged him for help. But once
you possess what your heart craves—then he
offers to give what you no longer want.   850
Would that be kindness? Fulfillment like that
is worthless—as are your offers to me.
They sound good, but in fact they're evil.

Let me explain your motives to these men,
so they'll see just how treacherous you are.

You have sought me out—not to take me home—
but to plant me outside your borders,
so that your city will emerge unscathed
from any invasion launched against it.
You won't get *that*, but you'll get something else: 860
this part of me—my *spirit*—ravaging
your country. And it will rage there always:
my sons will inherit from their father
only enough of my homeland to die in!

Don't you see? I know the future of Thebes
better than you do. A great deal better,
because my sources are better: Apollo,
for instance, and his father, Zeus himself.
Your lying mouth has come here spitting out
all those words—your tongue's keener than a blade.   870
But your guile hurts you far more than it helps.

I don't think I've persuaded you. So leave!
Let me live here! Poor as I am, I won't
live in want if I'm at peace with myself.

KREON

In our exchange, who do you think suffers
more, *me* by your views, or *you* by your own?

OEDIPUS

All that matters to me is that you've failed
to change my mind, or the minds of these men.

KREON

Growing old hasn't improved your judgment,
friend. It's perpetuated your disgrace.   880

OEDIPUS

Your tongue's extremely quick. But a good man
never pleads a dishonorable cause.

KREON

Making noise doesn't prove you're making sense.

OEDIPUS

As if *you* spoke briefly, and to the point?

KREON

Not pointedly enough to pierce your mind.

OEDIPUS

Go! I speak for these men and for myself.
Don't keep me under hostile surveillance
in a land that's destined to be my home.

KREON gestures toward the OLD MEN *and his Soldiers.*

KREON

I ask *these* men—not you—and I ask my . . .
comrades here, to note the tone you're taking   890
with a kinsman. If I ever seize you . . .

OEDIPUS

Who could seize me against my friends' will?

KREON

I swear you'll suffer even if we don't.

OEDIPUS

How do you plan to back up your bluster?

KREON

I've already seized one of your daughters
and removed her. I'll take the other soon.

OEDIPUS

My god.

KREON

Soon you'll have greater cause to say, "My god."

OEDIPUS

You took Ismene?

KREON

                    And I'll soon take this one.

KREON indicates ANTIGONE.

OEDIPUS

What will *you* do, my hosts—my friends?   900
Fail me by not banishing
this blaspheming thug?

LEADER

(to KREON)

Stranger, go. There's no way to justify
what you're attempting, or what you've just done.

KREON

(to his Soldiers)

It's time we take this girl away, by force
if she puts up the slightest resistance.

ANTIGONE

I don't know where to run. Are there men
or gods willing to help me?

LEADER

                                   What are you doing, stranger?

KREON

I'll leave him, but I will take *her*. She's mine.

OEDIPUS

You men in power here!

LEADER

Stranger, there's no   910
justification for what you're doing.

KREON

I can justify it.

LEADER

How can you do that?

KREON

I'm taking what belongs to me.

KREON grabs ANTIGONE.

OEDIPUS

Stop him, Athens!

LEADER

What is this, stranger? Let the daughter go—
or you'll discover who holds power here.

KREON

Stand back!

LEADER

Not from you! Not while you do this!

KREON

Touch me, and you're at war with Thebes.

OEDIPUS

All of this I foresaw.

LEADER

                    Release the girl.

KREON

Don't issue orders when you have no power.

LEADER

I warn you, let her go.

KREON

                    And I warn you: leave!   920

LEADER

(yelling offstage)
Over here, citizens! Join our fight! My city,
our city, is attacked! Come help us!

ANTIGONE

They're dragging me away! Friends! FRIENDS!

OEDIPUS

Where are you, child?

ANTIGONE

                    ... I ... can't ... get ... free!

OEDIPUS

Reach out to me, daughter.

ANTIGONE

They are too strong.

KREON

(to his Soldiers)

Take her away from here.

ANTIGONE

                        I'm so weak! So weak! I can't stop them.

KREON's Soldiers drag ANTIGONE offstage.

KREON

Now you won't have two daughters for crutches.
But since you want to lay waste your country
and its people—who've ordered me to do this,
though I remain their king—go right ahead,   930
fight for victory! You will find that nothing
you're doing now, nothing you've ever done,
has done you any good—you've turned your back
on those who love you, while they've tried
to stop your self-destructive fury.

LEADER

Stop where you are, stranger.

LEADER grabs hold of KREON.

KREON
Keep your hands off me.

LEADER
When you've brought back his daughters!

KREON
That will cost Thebes a much steeper ransom.
I'll take something worth more than these two girls.   940

LEADER
What are you threatening?

LEADER lifts his hands from KREON.

KREON
                              To seize that man there.

LEADER
Those are shocking words.

KREON
                              But ones I'll make good.

LEADER
You might—unless our king stops you.

OEDIPUS

That is outrageous! So you would seize me?

KREON

Shut up!

OEDIPUS

     NO!
           Goddesses, don't gag
the curse rising in my throat—on you, scum,
who have stolen my dear defenseless eyes,
gone like the sight I once possessed.
Let the Sun, who sees all there is, give you,
and every member of your family,   950
an old age as miserable as my own.

KREON

You people who live here, do you see that?

OEDIPUS

They see us both. They know you have caused me
real harm, while I've struck back with mere breath.

KREON

I will not curb my rage! Though I'm alone,
though age enfeebles me, I will take him.

KREON takes hold of OEDIPUS.

OEDIPUS

He's done it.

LEADER

Stranger, what arrogance possessed you?
You think you can accomplish this?

KREON

I *will* accomplish it.   960

LEADER

Then I'll cease to believe Athens is a city.

KREON

The weak overcome the powerful
if they have justice on their side.

OEDIPUS

                    Did you hear him?

LEADER

Zeus, back me up! He can't enforce his boast.

KREON

But Zeus knows that I can. And you don't know.

LEADER

That's an outrage!

KREON

                    An outrage you can't stop.

LEADER

You men who govern us! Come here! Be quick!
These men are heading for the border.

Enter THESEUS and his Men. KREON releases OEDIPUS and steps back.

THESEUS

What makes you shout? What's wrong?
Are you so panicked that you'll disrupt   970
my sacrifice to the seagod of Kolonos?
Speak up! Tell me the whole story, so I'll
know why I've run here so fast my legs ache.

OEDIPUS

I recognize your voice, friend. That man
over there has done me serious harm.

THESEUS

What harm? Which man?

OEDIPUS

Kreon. He's right there, you see him. He's taken
two of my children—the two I have left.

THESEUS

What are you saying?

OEDIPUS

I've told you what he did.

THESEUS

Someone run to my people at the altars.   980
Order every man there to leave the sacrifice
and converge at the crossroads. Go on foot,
or loosen your horses' reins and make them
gallop. Stop those girls from leaving town,
so I won't look useless to this stranger,
caught off guard by a desperate act. Go now!
And as for that man standing over there—
if I could punish him for what he's done
there is no way he would ever go free.
As things stand, he's protected by the laws   990
that authorized his visit to Athens.

(to KREON)

But we won't turn you loose until you bring
the girls here, where I can see them. Your actions
shame me, your family, and your country.

You've come to a city that loves justice.
We will do nothing contrary to law,
even though you flout our laws—invading
our territory, grabbing what you please,
keeping it by force. Do you think no men,
only slaves, live here? That I don't matter?   1000
It's not your breeding that makes you
a vile man. Thebes does not breed criminals.

She wouldn't support you, not if she knew
you were plundering what belongs to me—
and to the gods—using force to abduct
helpless suppliants.

                If I had crossed
your borders, no matter how just my cause,
I would first ask your ruler's agreement,
whoever he might be, before I dragged
anybody off. I'd know how a stranger   1010
should deal with your country's citizens.
But you've given your city a bad name
it doesn't deserve. And as you've grown old
the years have blighted your intelligence.

I said before, and I say now: Someone
must bring the girls back. Unless you'd like
to take up permanent residence here.
These aren't just words. They speak my mind.

LEADER

Do you see what's become of you, stranger?
We thought at first that you were honest—like   1020
your people. Now we see the harm you cause.

KREON

I didn't take these actions assuming,
as you would have it, that this city lacked
brave or intelligent men. I took them
because I assumed that its people

were not so taken with my relatives
as to feed and house them against my will.
I was sure you people wouldn't shelter
a morally toxic father-killer,
a man whose wife bore children to her son.   1030

I knew that the Council of Mount Ares
convenes in your city, and believed it
much too wise to let vagrants enter Athens.
I trusted my conviction when I seized him.
Nor would I have abducted him
if he hadn't laid curses on my kinfolk.
I am a man maligned! I have a right
to strike back. Anger doesn't diminish
as we age. It consumes us till we die.
Only the dead are immune from anguish.   1040

Do what you want with me.
Though I'm nothing, mine is a just cause.
I may be old, but I'll attempt
to pay you back blow for blow.

OEDIPUS

You have no shame! Tell me, does your nonsense
about a weak old man best fit you? Or me?
You charge me with murder, incest, disgrace—
misfortunes I suffered, but none of which
I chose. Perhaps it pleased the gods to hate
my ancestors. Examine my whole life.   1050

You can accuse me of no personal
wrongdoing, no crime whose expiation
impelled me to harm myself and my kin.

Tell me this. If the oracle of god
had decreed my father must die
at the hands of his own son, how
could you possibly think it just
to blame me? I wasn't even born!
No father had begotten me,
no mother had conceived me.   1060

And if, born to this miserable fate
as I most surely was, I traded blows
with my father in combat, and killed him,
not knowing what I was doing, or to whom—
how could you condemn that ignorant act?
As for my mother—you disgrace yourself
when you force me to speak of her marriage.
She was your sister, and our marriage
happened in just the way I'll now describe.
Given what's come from your vulgar mouth,   1070
there is no reason to shut mine.

Yes!—she bore me. And that wrecked both our lives.
I didn't know the truth, neither did she.
She give birth to me, and then she give birth
to children I fathered—to her shame.

I'm certain of one thing: it is your own
free choice to condemn us. But was my will
free when I married her? No! Nor do I
have any choice but to speak of it now.
Neither my marriage, nor the killing   1080
of my father—actions you keep on
throwing in my face—can be called crimes.

Of all my questions, answer just this one:
if, right now, a man standing beside you—
righteous you—tried to kill you, would you ask
whether or not the would-be murderer
was your father, or would you strike him down?
If your life mattered to you, I believe
you'd fight your assassin before you asked
yourself whether you were doing the right thing.   1090

Into such cataclysms the gods led me.
If my father's spirit came back to life,
I don't think he would disagree.

But you! Because you're not a moral man,
because you're willing to say anything,
because to you it's all the same—
speech that's vulgar and specch that's not—
you slander and defame me
in the presence of these good men.

You're quite happy to flatter Theseus—   1100
and Athens, for being such a well-run state.

Yet, in the midst of your adulation,
you have forgotten that if any city
knows the best way to venerate the gods,
it is Athens above all. So you try
to snatch me from this country, abuse me,
an old man, a suppliant! And worst of all
you seize my daughters! For all these reasons
I ask the goddesses living over there
for their help—provide me with friends!—so you   1110
may learn what kind of men defend this city.

LEADER

He's a good man, King. His destiny
may horrify us, but he's earned our help.

THESEUS

Enough discussion! The abductors
and their captives are on the move, while we,
the injured parties, just stand here.

KREON

What will you force a weak old man to do?

THESEUS

You can show me their route. I'll go with you.
If you're holding the girls we're searching for
nearby, you'll take me there yourself—but if   1120
your men have galloped off with their prizes,
that will save us some trouble, for my horsemen
will ride them down. Your men, thank god,

could never outrun mine to the frontier.
Let's go! Listen to me: the snake's defanged.
Fate's caught the marauder in her trap.
Whatever you win by cunning, you will lose.
You'll also lose your partners in this outrage.
I doubt you would have dared to attack us
unless you had some armed accomplices—   1130
perhaps you were counting on some traitor.
I'd better look to it—or else one lone
man could overthrow the whole city.
Are you hearing me? Or will you
ignore my words like the warnings you had
while you were planning this atrocity?

KREON

You're on home ground, so nothing you can say
disturbs me. Back in Thebes I'll know what to do.

THESEUS

Threaten me all you like—but start walking.
Oedipus, stay here. I'm sure you'll be safe.   1140
And I promise you this: unless I'm killed
I'll bring both of your daughters back alive.

OEDIPUS

May the gods bless your kindness, Theseus.
Bless your devotion to our welfare.

Exit THESEUS and his Men, escorting KREON.

OLD MEN

Oh let us be there,
to see the enemy
turn and fight! Bronze banging
bronze on the Pythian shore
or on torch-lit beaches
where two great queens—lips sworn   1150
to unbreakable silence
by the priests of Eumolpos—
nurture and watch over
funeral rites for the dead.
Out where Theseus,
the battle-igniter, and two
young girls, captive sisters,
converge at our borders,
surrounded by shouting
soldiers sure they have won.   1160
Or will the thieves be run down
in pastures west of the snowy
rock in the town of Oea,
as they flee on fast horses
or chariots driven at speed?
Kreon is beaten!
Men from Kolonos
make powerful warriors!
The steel of every bridle
flashes, the mounted troop   1170
charges ahead at full gallop.
They worship Athena;

they worship Poseidon,
the ocean-embracing
son of the goddess Rhea.

Are they in action yet,
or do they hold back?
My heart gives me
hope that the girls,
harshly tested,   1180
brutally abused
at the hands of their uncle,
will soon see us, face to face.

Today! Today is the day that Zeus
will conclude a great work,
the victory in battle I foresee!
Were I a dove right now, the storm's
thrust lifting my strong wings,
I might soar through a cloud,
the battle raging below me.   1190

Hear it, Zeus, who rules
all other gods, who sees
all that there is to see!
Let our country's defenders
strike the decisive blow
that will bring the prize home.
Help us, fearsome Athena!
Come, huntsman Apollo,

bring Artemis, your sister!
Come all you trackers   1200
of the dappled fast-moving deer—
help this land and our people!
You won't find me a false prophet,
wandering friend. I'm looking now
at the girls and their escort coming home.

OEDIPUS

Where? Can you tell me? What are you saying?

Enter ANTIGONE and ISMENE with THESEUS and his Men.

ANTIGONE

(from a distance)
Father!—if only some god would show you
this princely man who's brought us back to you!

OEDIPUS

Daughter? Is it you?

ANTIGONE

                    Yes! All these strong arms—
the king and his loyal men—set us free.   1210

OEDIPUS

Come toward me, child. Returned to me,
after I had lost hope. Come to my arms.

ANTIGONE

You ask for what I want to give.

OEDIPUS

Where are you, child?

ANTIGONE

We're both coming to you.

OEDIPUS embraces his daughters.

OEDIPUS

My darling children!

ANTIGONE

You love us all.

OEDIPUS

You strengthen my old frame.

ANTIGONE

And share your grief.

OEDIPUS

I hold all my dear ones. If I die now,
I won't die totally wretched, so long
as you two hold me like this. Cling so hard
you graft yourselves to your father, so tight   1220
I'll feel released at last from the wanderings
that have left me bone-tired and miserable.

Now tell me quickly what happened out there.
A girl your size should keep it short.

ANTIGONE

The man who saved us is right here.
It was all his doing. Let him tell it.
That's as brief as I can make it.

OEDIPUS

Don't be surprised, my friend, that I've spoken
so long and so intently to my daughters.
I was quite sure they were lost forever.   1230
I owe the joy I'm feeling now
to you. You freed them, no one else.

May the gods grant all that I wish for you—
both you and your city—for I've found you
the most god-fearing, evenhanded
people on Earth. And your tongues never lie.
I know your virtues. Let me honor them:
you—and no other—gave me what I have.

Please reach your right hand out to me, King,
so I may hold it and then kiss your face,   1240
if that's allowed.
                    What am I asking for?
Ill-omened creature that I've been since birth—
why should I want you to touch someone
like me—steeped in every evil?

No, I can't let you do it, not even
if you wished it. Those who have lived through
misery the same as my own, only they
may touch me. Take my salute where you stand.
As for the future, treat me justly.
Just as you've done so far.   1250

THESEUS

I'm not surprised you've spoken at such length,
elated as you are at your daughters' return,
or that you wanted to speak first with them.
Nothing like that would ever annoy me.
I want my life to shine through my actions,
not through my words. The proof, old man, is this:
I've kept my promises to you—brought back
unharmed both your stolen daughters.
How did we win the skirmish? Why should I
bother with that? Your daughters will tell you.   1260

But something happened just as I returned.
Perhaps you could advise me about it.
A small matter, but a surprising one,
and even small things shouldn't be ignored.

OEDIPUS

Son of Aigeus, what is this small thing?
Please tell me. I don't know why you're asking.

THESEUS

They tell me a man—your kinsman, but not
one from your city—lies on his stomach,
a suppliant at Poseidon's altar,
where I sacrificed before I set out.   1270

OEDIPUS

What country is he from? What does he want?

THESEUS

They tell me he wishes to speak briefly
with you. Nothing very consequential.

OEDIPUS

Speak of what? No one asks a god's help lightly.

THESEUS

He prayed, I'm told, for a meeting with you—
from which he'd be allowed to leave unharmed.

OEDIPUS

Who'd make an appeal like that to the god?

THESEUS

Do you recall having a kinsman in Argos—
someone who might ask you for help?

OEDIPUS

Friend, don't say any more.

THESEUS

What's wrong with you?   1280

OEDIPUS

Don't question me.

THESEUS

Not ask you what? Say it!

OEDIPUS

From what you've said, I know this suppliant.

THESEUS

But why should he offend me? Who is he?

OEDIPUS

King, he's my son. I hate him. His voice would
give me more pain than any other man's.

THESEUS

How so? Can't you listen, but do nothing
you don't wish to? Is it harmful to listen?

OEDIPUS

His voice itself is loathsome to me, King.
Don't compel me to do what you're asking.

THESEUS

You had better consider this: 1290
aren't you compelled by his

suppliant status? Haven't you
a solemn duty to honor the god?

ANTIGONE

Father, please hear me, even though I'm young
to give advice. Respect the king's conscience—
let him honor his god the way he must!
And for your daughters' sake, let our brother
come here. No matter how he maligns you,
he can't force you to change your mind, can he?
Hear what he has to say. What's wrong with that?   1300

You are his father, and you know that even
if he blames you in the most ungodly
vicious way, to do him wrong can't be right.
Show him compassion! Other fathers
afflicted with bad children, and just as short-
tempered as you, have softened in response
to the calming influence of their loved ones.
Look at your own past, and remember how
your parents' misery became your own.
And when you consider how theirs happened,   1310
I think you'll see that the surest outcome
of any evil you inflict—is more evil.

Please change your mind. It's not right for someone
pleading a just cause to plead it forever!
Or for a man who has been given help
to hesitate when asked to repay it.

OEDIPUS

Your arguments are winning me over,
daughter. Though what makes you happy
devastates me, I'll do what you ask.
(turning to THESEUS)
But if you let that man come here,   1320
my friend, no one, at any time,
must be given power over my life.

THESEUS

I wouldn't want to hear you repeat that,
old man. I never boast, but believe me,
as long as the gods let me live, you're safe.

Exit THESEUS and his Men.

OLD MEN

Anyone who craves
all the years he can have,
expecting to enjoy
a lifespan longer
than normal, makes,   1330
we promise you,
a foolish choice.

For the days that stretch out ahead
hold more sorrow than joy,
and the body whose limbs
once gave you pleasure

will soon give you none,
when you've lived past your prime.
And when the Caregiver comes,
he ends all lives the same way.   1340
Hades is suddenly real—
no lyre, no dancing, no marriage-song.
There is nothing but Death.

By any measure, it is best
never to have been born.
But once a man is born,
the next best thing, by far,
is for him to return,
as soon as he can,
to the place he came from.   1350
For once youth—with its mindless
indulgence—goes by, is there a single
punishing blow that won't find him?
Any misfortune that doesn't
attack his life? Envy, feuding,
revolt, battle, and murder!
And finally, old age: despised,
decrepit, lonely, friendless old age
takes him in—there he keeps house
with the worst of all evils.   1360

(looking toward OEDIPUS)

He too has arrived at those years,
that ruin of a man—we're not alone.
He's like some headland facing north,

lashed by the huge waves of winter.
He too is battered by the troubles
breaking over him, billows pounding in
from both the rising and the setting sun—
from the south, where it's noon all day long,
and from the black northern mountains.

ANTIGONE

I think a stranger's about to arrive.   1370
Just one lone man, Father. And he's in tears.

OEDIPUS

Who is he?

Enter a distraught, weeping POLYNEIKES.

ANTIGONE

The one we've been discussing:
Polyneikes. He's here.

POLYNEIKES

What should I do? Feel sorry for myself?
Or for the frail father I'm looking at?
I find him banished to a foreign country—
along with you two—living in rancid
rags for so long they've bonded to his flesh
like some disease. And his unruly hair   1380
snarls in the wind over his blinded face.
Just as miserable are the rations
he carries to feed his aching belly.

POLYNEIKES walks over to address OEDIPUS.

It shames me to have learned this so late.
I'll admit it: in all that touches
your welfare I've been wholly
irresponsible. But you're hearing this
from my mouth, not from anyone else's.
Father, you know that the goddess Respect
joins every action that Zeus takes. May she   1390
inspire you! I can atone for my sins;
I can't possibly make them any worse.

POLYNEIKES pauses for a response; OEDIPUS is silent.

You're quiet, father. Why? Please speak to me.
Don't turn your back. You won't respond at all?
Will you deny me with silent contempt?
You'll give no explanation for your rage?
My sisters! His daughters! Please make him talk.
Break through his sullen, stony silence.
Stop him from disdaining me like this.
I have the god's protection, yet this man   1400
turns me away without a single word.

ANTIGONE

Then tell him what you came for! You coward!
If you speak freely you might give him pleasure.
Try glowing with anger or affection.
Maybe then this mute man will find a voice.

POLYNEIKES

That was harsh but just. I *will* speak
plainly. But first I must ask help—of the god
from whose altar the king of this country
pulled me up, so I could come make my case,
hear yours, and be granted safe conduct   1410
to go my way. I hope I can trust you—
Father, Sisters—to honor those assurances.

I want to tell you why I'm here, Father.
I've been forced to flee my own country, exiled
after I claimed, as the elder son, my right
to inherit your throne and your power.
Eteokles, although my junior, expelled me.
He hadn't beaten me in court or tested
his strength against mine in battle, but he
somehow persuaded Thebes to back him.   1420

It's likely that the Fury who stalks you
strengthened his case. At least, that's what I'm told
by the omen-readers.
                         Soon after I arrived
in Argos I married King Adrastos'
daughter. That won me the support,
by a sworn oath, of the most battle-proven
warriors on the Peloponnesus, men
who would help me raise seven companies
of spearmen to fight Thebes, ready to die
for my cause—or drive out the vile rebels   1430
from our land.

           Why do I come here now?
I bring prayers, Father, my own, and those
of my allies—seven columns, seven
poised spears surrounding Thebes on all sides.
Quick-thrusting Amphiaraos joins me,
unmatched in battle or in prophecy,
then Oineus' son, Tydeus,
from Aitolia. The third, Eteoklos,
comes from Argos. Fourth is Hippomedon,
sent by his father, Talaos. The fifth one,   1440
Kapaneus, promises he'll use fire
to burn down Thebes. Parthenopaios,
named after his mother, the aging virgin
Atalanta, whose late marriage produced him,
hurries to war from Arcadia.

And I, your son—or if I'm not really
your son, but the spawn of an evil fate,
at least I'm yours according to my name—
I lead Argos' brave army against Thebes.

All of us, father—for your children's sake,   1450
for the sake of your own life—beg you now
to give up your anger at me,
now that I'm ready to punish the brother
who banished me and robbed me of my country.

If what the oracles predict holds true,
victory will go to the side you join.
Now, in the name of the fountains of home,

in the name of our tribal gods, I ask you
to listen and relent. I'm a beggar,
an exile, but so are you. The kindness   1460
of others supports us both, and we share
a common fate—while he, that arrogant
dictator back in our homeland, mocks us
equally. But if you support me now,
I'll crush him soon and without much trouble.
When I've expelled him by force, I'll put you
back in your house, and myself back in power.
If you join me, I'll make good on that boast.
But if you don't help me, I'm a dead man.

LEADER

(sotto voce)

Respect the person who sent him to us,   1470
Oedipus. Say something expedient
to him—before you send him on his way.

OEDIPUS

No, my friends, you who oversee this grove:
if Theseus hadn't ordered him here,
believing me obliged to answer him,
he would never have heard me raise my voice.
But now, before he goes, he'll feel that blessing.
And he will hear from me some things
that won't make him happy:

(suddenly turning on POLYNEIKES)

There are no worse men than you!   1480

When you held the power your brother now holds
you made me an outcast with no city,
forced to wear the rags that bring tears to your eyes—
now that you're facing the same ordeal.
I've put tears behind me. As long as I live
I'll bear the burden of knowing that you
would have killed me. You made me swallow filth,
you drove me out, and you made me a foul
tramp who begs his daily bread from strangers!
Had I not begotten caring daughters   1490
I'd be dead—for all the help you gave me.

These two girls keep me alive. They nurse me.
When the work's hard, they're men, not women.
You're not my sons, you're someone else's sons,
alien to me.
                    Right now, Fate watches you,
but not as it soon will, when your soldiers
march on Thebes. You won't destroy Thebes. You'll die.
The blood you shed will defile you, just as
your blood defiles your brother as he dies.

I cursed you both from my heart long ago.   1500
I summon those same curses to help me
fight you now, to impress you with the need
to respect your parents and not to treat
your father with contempt—a sightless man
who begot the kind of men you became.
Your sisters never disgraced me!

                         My curses

will overpower your prayers and your thrones—
if Justice still sits there, alongside Zeus,
enforcing the laws of our ancestors.

As for you now, clear out! I spit on you!   1510
I'm not your father, you despicable
bastard! And don't forget to take with you
the curses I have called down on your head—
you'll never win this war on your homeland.
You won't survive to skulk back to the plains
of Argos. By your brother's hand you will
die—as you'll kill the man who threw you out.
That is my curse: and I ask the blackest
paternal darkness of the underworld
to become your new home in Tartaros.   1520
I summon the spirits native to this place.
I summon Ares the Destroyer, who has
inflamed your minds with murderous hatred!

Now that you've heard this, go tell Thebes, go
tell all your staunch allies, what a great favor
Oedipus has done for his own two sons.

LEADER

Polyneikes, this account of your life
gives me no pleasure. And now, you should go.

POLYNEIKES

So much for my journey and my wrecked hopes.
So much for my fellow soldiers. What a way   1530
to end our march from Argos! I'm finished!
There is no way I can tell my army
what happened here. Retreat? Out of the question.
I must face my destiny in silence.
My sisters, his daughters, since you've heard
my father's savage curse, promise me this:
if that curse does come true and you manage
to make your way home, don't dishonor me,
but bury me. Perform the rituals.
You've already won praise for the loyal   1540
care you've given this man, but you will earn
equal praise for the honor you show me.

ANTIGONE

Polyneikes, I've got to change your mind.

POLYNEIKES

About what, dear Sister? Tell me, Antigone.

ANTIGONE

Turn your army around. Go back to Argos.
Do it now. Don't destroy yourself and Thebes.

POLYNEIKES

That's something I can't do. How could I lead
my troops out here again, once I'd shown fear?

ANTIGONE

Why would you renew your anger, Brother?
And what do you gain, razing your homeland?   1550

POLYNEIKES

Because I was disgraced, banished,
ridiculed, by my younger brother.

ANTIGONE

Don't you see, if you attack you'll fulfill
your father's prophecies—that you will both
kill each other?

POLYNEIKES

                    Isn't that what he wants?
Why shouldn't I obey him?

ANTIGONE

Listen to your wretched sister: who will
obey you, once they've heard his prophecies?

POLYNEIKES

Why should I tell them bad news? Skillful
generals report good news and censor bad.   1560

ANTIGONE

Oh my brother! You're absolutely determined?

POLYNEIKES

That's right. Please don't get in my way. My job
is to take that road, no matter what deadly
consequences Father predicts for me—
he and his Furies. But you two—I hope
Zeus will protect your future, so you can
carry out my wishes after I'm killed.
Let me leave—say goodbye. For you'll
never again see me alive.

POLYNEIKES pulls away from her arms.

ANTIGONE

This breaks my heart.

POLYNEIKES

Don't let it.

ANTIGONE

Who wouldn't feel grief for a brother   1570
when he's headed toward certain death?

POLYNEIKES

If that's my fate, then I must die.

ANTIGONE

Don't die. Please listen to me!

POLYNEIKES

You must stop this. My mind's made up.

ANTIGONE

And I am truly devastated.
Now that I'm sure I'll lose you.

POLYNEIKES

No, Fate will determine how my life goes.
I pray that you two never come to harm.
All men know that you don't deserve it.

Exit POLYNEIKES.

OLD MEN

We've just seen　　　　　　　　　　　　　　　1580
the blind stranger
start a new round
of deadly violence—
unless Fate working
its will is the true cause.
You'll never hear us declare
that a god wills something in vain:
for Time always keeps watch
over the gods' decrees—
ruining somebody's chances,　　　　　　　　　1590
then rescuing somebody else
the very next morning
when his turn comes.

A crash of thunder.

That was thunder! O Zeus!

OEDIPUS
Children! Children!
Is there someone nearby
who could bring Theseus?
There is no better man.

ANTIGONE
Father, why do we need Theseus here?

OEDIPUS
Because Zeus sends that thunder, and its great wings   1600
will carry me to Hades. Find him now.

More and louder thunder.

OLD MEN
Look, Zeus throws down
a great unspeakable
blast of fire!
Terror races
to the tips of my hair,
my spirit cowers,
the lightning strikes again—
crackles down the sky—
forcing what? To be born.   1610

I am afraid. Lightning never
erupts to no purpose, it always
portends something horrendous.
O mighty sky! O Zeus!

OEDIPUS

Daughters, the death promised to your father
is at hand. Nothing can stop it now.

ANTIGONE

How do you know? What warnings have you had?

OEDIPUS

It's beyond doubt. Quickly now, someone go
find the king and bring him back to me.

Another blast of thunder.

OLD MEN

Yes! Yes! Hear it! That voice of raging thunder   1620
is yet again all around us!
Be gentle with us, god, gentle—
if you are about to darken
our motherland.
Forgive us, if we've sheltered
a man you despise.
Don't punish our compassion!
I ask that of you, Zeus!

OEDIPUS

Is he nearby? Will he find me alive,
children, when he comes? Will my mind be clear?   1630

ANTIGONE

Why do you worry that your mind's unsound?

OEDIPUS

I promised I'd repay Theseus
for his kindness. Now I must give him
everything he has earned.

LEADER

(calling offstage)
You there, my son, we need you! Come!
Break off the sacrifice to seagod Poseidon,
leave the crevice among the high rocks
and come back! The stranger is moved
to provide you, your city, your friends,
with the fruits of your kindness to him.   1640
Move quickly, King.

Enter THESEUS and his Men.

THESEUS

What's all this noise,
this frantic summons—from both
my people and our guest?
Did Zeus' lightning upset you? Did

a hailstorm raise a sudden uproar?
A storm like that, when a god sends it,
inspires every kind of fear.

OEDIPUS

We're reassured, King, now that you've come.
A god's behind this good timing.   1650

THESEUS

What's happened, son of Laios?

OEDIPUS

My life is weighted to sink down.
I must not die without fulfilling
my guarantees to you and Athens.

THESEUS

What makes you think your death is imminent?

OEDIPUS

The gods themselves told me. Every sign
I was promised has now been given me.

THESEUS

Which sign made it entirely clear?

OEDIPUS

A great crash of thunder and bolts of lightning
flashing from the All-Powerful's hand.   1660

THESEUS

I believe you. You've made some prophecies,
not one of them false. What should I do now?

OEDIPUS

I will describe, son of Aigeus,
how the future of Athens will become
impervious to the ravages of time.
Soon, I myself, with no hand guiding me,
will lead you to the place where I must die.
Never reveal that place to anyone—
not how it's hidden, nor its whereabouts.
It will endure, an ever-present defense,   1670
more powerful than a rampart of shields,
or allies with spears racing to save you.

As for those mysteries speech would profane,
you will see what they are, once you are there,
alone. I will not reveal them now, not
to these people, not even to the children
I love. No, you must keep all those secrets.
When you're near death, tell them to your successor.
Let him teach his heir, and so on forever.

In this way, your own city will survive   1680
unscathed any attack launched by the Thebans.
Many cities, even well-governed cities,
slide smoothly into violence.
Though the gods act slowly, they see clearly

men who cease to believe and go mad.
Keep this from happening to you, son of Aigeus.

But you don't need such tutoring from me.
Now we must move toward that place,
for god's power drives me on.
Don't linger, follow where I lead.   1690
Daughters, in some uncanny way
I have become your guide, as you
once guided your father. Come with me, but
don't touch me with your hands, let me find
the sacred tomb with no help, and the ground
where it's my destiny to be buried.
This way. That's right. Through here. Down this path
my guide Hermes escorts me, he and the dark goddess.

OEDIPUS, *with uncanny ease, leads his daughters and* THESEUS *toward the*
grove, his voice still heard after he vanishes offstage. THESEUS, ANTIGONE,
and ISMENE, *one by one, follow* OEDIPUS *out of sight.*

O light—dark to me now,
though once you were mine—I feel   1700
your warmth on my body one last time.
I'm going down, to hide my death
in Hades. Come, dearest stranger:
bless you, bless this land, bless your people.
And in your prosperous state,
remember me when I am dead,
the source of your boundless well-being.

OLD MEN

If she, the unseen goddess,
accepts my solemn prayer,
and if you, god of the night people,   1710
will hear me out, Aidoneus, Aidoneus!
I pray you let this stranger go
untortured and undamned
down to the dark fields of the dead,
down to the house of Styx.
Troubles beyond reason
besieged him. In return
a just god shall pull him clear.

Earth Goddesses! And you,
invincible apparition!   1720
Savage guard-dog! Rumor
has told us for ages that you
kennel at Hades' gate, snarling

from cavernous jaws at every
stranger who walks past.
Hear me, Death!
Son of Earth and Tartaros!
Let the hound clear a path
for this stranger who craves
the sunken fields of the dead.   1730
Grant him eternal rest.

Enter MESSENGER.

MESSENGER

Townsmen, I could shorten my news to this:
Oedipus is gone. But the full story
of what happened out there cannot be cut short,
nor did the things themselves happen quickly.

LEADER

Is he dead—that tormented man?

MESSENGER

                              You can be sure
this man has left our common life behind.

LEADER

How? Did the gods take him? Did he feel pain?

MESSENGER

How it happened will take your breath away.
How he left, you saw. None of his loved ones   1740
knew the way, but he knew where to lead us.
As soon as he neared the gateway where you climb
down those steep brass steps rooted in the earth,
he paused—within a maze of crossing paths—
where a bowl had been hollowed from a rock shelf.
There the immortal pact that Theseus
made with Peirithous is written in stone.

He stood between that basin and the rock
of Thoricos, easing himself to the ground

beside a hollow pear trunk and a stone tomb.   1750
He peeled off all his filthy clothes, then called
to his daughters, asking them to bring water
from the stream nearby, so he could bathe
and then pour out some libations.
The green hill of Demeter rose close by
in plain sight. They climbed it, and soon
carried out these duties for their father.
First they washed him and then they dressed him
in white clothes customary for the dying.

When he was content with what had been done,   1760
every last one of his orders obeyed,
Zeus of the Underworld thundered, and the girls
shuddered when they heard it. Then, clinging
to their father's knees, they cried out and kept
pounding their breasts and weeping and shouting.
When he heard them crying, he wrapped his arms
around both their bodies and told them,
"Children, this day will end your father's life.
All the acts I lived for have come to pass.
No longer will you need to care for me—   1770
a burden, I know, that has not been easy.
But let one word relieve you of this hardship:
for no man loves you more than I love you.
Now you must live out your lives without me."

Holding each other close, all of them sobbed,
and when they had finished their lamenting,

as the sounds died away, there was stillness.
Suddenly an enormous voice called him,
making everyone's hair rise in terror.
For the god called many times and his voice   1780
echoed from all sides: "You there, Oedipus!
You! Oedipus! Why do we hesitate?
You've waited far too long. Far too long!"

Now that he knew it was the god calling,
he asked King Theseus to stand by him.
And when the king approached, Oedipus said,
"Dear friend, will you promise, by giving your
right hand to my daughters, while they give you
their hands, that you will never willingly
forsake them, and that you will always act   1790
as their friend, providing what they will need?"
And like a prince, with no hesitation,
Theseus swore to the stranger that he would.
And after this promise, Oedipus at once
embraced his children with enfeebled hands,
and said, "Daughters, you must have the courage
to leave this place now. Don't look back
at things you must not see, and must not hear.
Leave quickly as you can. Let Theseus,
who is entitled to do so, remain   1800
to witness all that will happen here."

That's what he said, we all heard him, and followed
his daughters as they left, tears blurring

our own eyes. When we had walked on awhile,
we looked back and saw he was gone, and saw
our king, his hand screening his eyes, reacting
to the shock of a terrifying sight, something
he could not bear to look at, something still
happening. A moment later, we saw him
silently saluting the Earth, then the sky   1810
where the Olympian gods live, his arms
opened in prayer.

              But the exact nature
of the death Oedipus died, no man
but Theseus could tell you. Zeus didn't
incinerate him with a lightning blast,
no sudden squall blew inland from the sea.
So it was either a god spiriting
him away, or else the Earth's lower world—
her deep foundations—opening to him,
for he felt nothing but welcoming kindness.   1820

When this man vanished, there was no sorrow.
He suffered no sickness. His death, like no
other man's, was a cause for wonder.
If anyone listening doesn't believe me,
I have no interest in persuading him
that I am not some credulous fool.

LEADER
Where are the girls and their escort now?

MESSENGER

Not far away. The sounds of their grief
growing louder tells you they're almost here.

ANTIGONE

(anguished cries)

No reason now   1830
for we two woeful sisters
to hold back the full
wretchedness that we feel—
the doomed blood of our father
flowed at birth into our blood.
As long as our father lived
we suffered its relentless agony.
Even from his last moments,
we take with us things seen and things
suffered that defy understanding.   1840

LEADER

What did you see?

ANTIGONE

Friends, we can only guess.

LEADER

Then he's gone?

ANTIGONE

In the very way you'd wish—
because it wasn't the war god or the waves,

it was the endless marsh of death that drew
him away, in a weird, sudden vanishing.
And now, Sister, there's a deathly darkness
clouding our vision—for how can we stand
our harsh life to come, drifting across some
remote back country, or over breaking seas?   1850

ISMENE

I don't know. I'd rather murderous Hades
forced me to share my agèd father's death.
I'm shaking. I can't face the life ahead.

LEADER

You two sisters,
loving daughters,
accept what the god brings.
Do not inflame yourselves
with so much grieving.
You should not regret
the path your life took.   1860

ANTIGONE

Yes, there was something
to treasure in our pain.
What gave me no comfort then
did, in the end, console me.
Yes it did—while I held him
lovingly in my arms.
Dear Father, loved one, you
will wear Earth's darkness

forever, but even down there
you won't be denied   1870
my love and her love.

LEADER

Then what took place . . .

ANTIGONE

                                    . . . was what he desired.

LEADER

How so?

ANTIGONE

To die on foreign earth
was his wish. He will sleep
in that dark grave forever.
And the mourners he left
behind are not dry-eyed.
With my own eyes pouring
I grieve for you, Father.   1880
I don't know how to stop,
my ache is so huge.
I know your wish was to die
in a distant country.
But now you have died
bereft of my care.

ISMENE

Poor desolate Sister,
what will come of us both,
now that Father is gone?

LEADER

Since the way he met death   1890
was a blessing, children,
stop grieving. Not one of us
escapes misfortune.

ANTIGONE

Sister, we must go back there.

ISMENE

To do what?

ANTIGONE

I'm filled with . . .

ISMENE

With what?

ANTIGONE

. . . longing. To see the earthly resting place . . .

ISMENE

Whose?

ANTIGONE

Our father's!   1900

ISMENE

Such a thing can't possibly
be right. Can't you see that?

ANTIGONE

Why are you judging me?

ISMENE

There's one more thing that you don't know . . .

ANTIGONE

What will you tell me next?

ISMENE

No one saw him die! There's no tomb!

ANTIGONE

Take me out there, and kill me too.

ISMENE

That would kill *me*! With no friends and no strength,
where would I live out my deserted life?

LEADER

Children, you have nothing to fear.   1910

ANTIGONE

Then where can we go?

LEADER

We know of a refuge . . .

ANTIGONE

What do you mean?

LEADER

. . . where you'll be safe.

ANTIGONE

I think I know it . . .

LEADER

What are you thinking?

ANTIGONE

I don't see how we can go home.

LEADER

Then I don't think you should try.

ANTIGONE

Trouble pursues us.

LEADER

It has from the start.   1920

ANTIGONE

It was horrible. Now it's worse.

LEADER

Your life has been a huge sea of hardship.

ANTIGONE

So it has.

Enter THESEUS with his Men.

THESEUS

Stop weeping, children. When the Earth Powers
have shown all of us so much grace,
grief is uncalled for. Don't anger them.

ANTIGONE

Son of Aigeus, please help us.

THESEUS

What do you want me to do, children?

ANTIGONE

Let us see Father's tomb with our own eyes.

THESEUS

That would violate divine law.   1930

ANTIGONE

What do you mean, my lord?

THESEUS

Daughters, his orders were to let no one
approach that place, to let no one
speak to the sacred tomb where he's sleeping.
If I keep my word, this land
will never be harmed. Horkos,
the servant of Zeus
who hears all oaths,
heard mine. He misses nothing.

ANTIGONE

I'm content, if my father's wishes   1940
are fulfilled. Now send us home
to prevent, if we can, the slaughter
that threatens our brothers.

THESEUS

I will do that. I'll give you all the help
you may need: anything the dead man,
now gone under the earth, would approve.

LEADER

Stop mourning now. Let it be. In all
that's happened, there's nothing you can change.

ALL leave.

NOTES TO THE PLAY

2 *Have we come to a town?* It's clear from the exchange at
28–29 that Oedipus and Antigone know they're approach-
ing Athens. Oedipus wants to know both what place (*koros*)
or piece of open ground they're near and what town (*polis*).
The word *polis* normally means city, but here it more likely
refers to a smaller inhabited entity. The eventual answer to
Oedipus' last question is: Kolonos.

11 *on public land, or in a grove* Oedipus is so tired that he
doesn't care whether he and Antigone rest in a public space
or risk trespassing, which they will shortly do, into a sacred grove (or precinct) from which unauthorized folk are
excluded.

23 *nightingales* Nightingales symbolize death. This is the first
allusion to the "holy place" where Oedipus will die.

25 *Be my lookout* Antigone maintains a sentinel's alertness
throughout, spotting in turn the Stranger, the Old Men, Ismene, Kreon, and Polyneikes just before each enters.

37 *Stranger* The word *xenos*, translated usually throughout the
text as "stranger," can also mean, and is sometimes translated as, "host" or "guest" depending on the context. The
character called the Stranger in the surviving texts would
most probably be a local farmer.

44–50 *fearsome goddesses . . . harsher names* The fearsome goddesses (literally, *emphoboi theai*) are the Eumenides, chthonian (or Earth) powers associated with death and the underworld (as opposed to Olympian, the heavenly or sky gods). Originally known as the Erinys, or Furies, they avenge wrongs done to family members—disrespect for elders, for instance, but especially kin murder. They were worshipped under a variety of names. Thebans, including Oedipus in this play, address them as "Ladies." In Athens their cult name was "Solemn Ones" (*Semnai*). Those who called them Kindly Ones did so to deflect their ire. In 50 (literally, "other places have different names"), I translate the euphemistic "different" as "harsher" to highlight the Stranger's subtext, which is that these goddesses are dangerous. See note to 92.

51 *suppliant* Oedipus claims his formal status as a suppliant, one who makes a specific request of a higher authority, usually a god or his representative, or a ruler. Suppliants generally expected and were granted divine protection, though there were horrific exceptions, particularly during times of war or civil strife, in which suppliants were granted safety and then slaughtered.

54 here *is where I meet my fate* Oedipus' words in Greek are compact and mysterious. They may also be translated: "It's the sign of my destiny." The Greek word *synthema*, if translated literally as "sign," means a particular agreed-upon token, signal, or code word (Jebb 1986, 19). Oedipus could be saying that the name "Eumenides" is the sign foretold to him by Apollo's priestess at Delphi. Or he could mean that his intended prayer or the grove itself is the sign. In any case,

Apollo had promised that when Oedipus arrived at the grove of the Eumenides he would find rest at last. When Oedipus suddenly hears the name of the presiding goddesses, "the Kindly Ones," he turns brusquely decisive. He's arrived on promised ground and will not be moved.

62–64 *This entire grove . . . shrine here* Sacred groves in ancient Greece could harbor more than one divinity. This grove's major god is Poseidon, whose affinity with horses and the sea made him important to the Athenians, since navy and cavalry were crucial to their military prowess. The grove also contains shrines to Prometheus, and to the Eumenides, the grove's resident deities described in the note to 44–50.

65 *brass-footed threshold* In Sophocles' era, a well-known grove was located in Kolonos about a mile north of the Acropolis on the main route into Athens. Somewhere near the grove was a steeply descending rift or cavern in the rock, perhaps reinforced with brass to forms "steps." Jebb calls them "the *stay* of Athens: a phrase in which the idea of a physical basis is joined to that of a religious safeguard" (1886, 57n). The ancient audience would have understood the grove's rich mythical and historical associations and connected them to the area "on stage." See notes 1746–47 and 1748–50.

68 *We've all taken his name* Inhabitants commonly added their hometowns to their given names; e.g., Sophocles of Kolonos; Ion of Chios.

76 *Theseus* Theseus was a legendary hero who arrived in Athens as a formidable teenager after killing many human and bestial adversaries on the way from his birthplace in Troezen. He was unaware that the reigning king of Athens

was actually his father, Aigeus (though in some versions of the myth Poseidon had actually sired him). Theseus' great political accomplishment was the unification of Attica under Athenian leadership.

81 *My words . . . can see* Oedipus claims here only the immediate cogency of his speech, but his confident assertion suggests the prophetic power his words will acquire and project during the course of the play.

84 *down on your luck* Literally, *daimon*, a personal deity who directs the events of an individual's life. At this point the Stranger doesn't realize the full implication of the *daimon* impacting Oedipus' life. See introduction to *Oedipus the King* passim.

92 *eyes we dread* Literally, *deinopes*, or "dread-eyed." The Kindly Ones were dreaded for their power to "see everything," especially all kinds of malfeasance. That power enabled them to detect and punish intrafamilial abuse.

95 *Apollo* Apollo, one of the twelve Olympian gods, was a symbol of light and sometimes associated with Helios, god of the sun. Apollo's primary epithet, *Phoibos*, means "shining." He also oversaw the sites, the practice, and the profession of prophecy. As revealed in *Oedipus the King*, Apollo's priestess, the Pythoness at Delphi, prophesied Oedipus' fate: that Oedipus would kill his father and marry his mother.

107–108 *sober man . . . spurn wine* Most Greek divinities received wine as an offering; the Eumenides were an exception. While Oedipus' sobriety might result from the recent austere circumstances of his life, it also alludes to the frightening countenance he shares with the goddesses. See note to 155.

127–187 *Look for him . . . keep quiet* These lines comprise the *parodos* or entry song of the chorus, or Old Men, and like the choral odes to follow, were sung and accompanied by an oboe-like instrument, the *aulos*. This entry song is unusual in its utilitarian purpose; instead of reporting an event, it enacts an event: the search for and discovery of the grove's invader. The Old Men operate here and later as "security guards" who protect the sacred grove and the community of Kolonos. Oedipus addresses them as "guardians."

147–151 *We've heard . . . hiding place* The Leader and the Old Men, by interchangeably referring to themselves as "I" or "we," reinforce their collective nature.

155 *The sight of you . . . appalls us* Literally, "dreadful" [*deinos*] to see, dreadful to hear." Oedipus used the word *deinos* to refer to the Eumenides at 92.

234 *The horror I was born to* Oedipus' life. He refers to the fate assigned him before birth by Apollo, a fate he began living as soon as he was born.

242–244 *Laios' son . . . house of Labdakos* Laios was Oedipus' father, the man he killed without knowing his true identity; Labdakos, an earlier king of Thebes, was Laios' father.

259–260 *burden / our city . . . deadly contagion* Literally, "place a heavy obligation on the city." The obligation here is a *miasma*, or pollution. Ancient Greeks believed that those who murdered blood kin carried with them a contagion that would inflict damage on those in contact with the murderer. At the beginning of *Oedipus the King*, Thebes suffers from such a contagion, which causes deadly disease, crop failure, and rampant miscarriage.

287–288 *Athens . . . haven for persecuted strangers* Athens'
reputation as a haven for exiles in distress was prominent in
myth and the dramas derived from myth. Athens sheltered
Orestes when he was pursued by the Furies; both the children of Herakles, who were persecuted by King Eurystheus;
and the crazed Herakles himself after he had murdered his
wife and children. Athens maintained that reputation in
Sophocles' era by welcoming and granting legal status to
immigrants as *metics*, allowing them to work and take part
in some civic activities.

303–304 *those who tried / to murder me* Oedipus here refers
to Jokasta and Laios, his true parents. When they heard
an oracle's prophecy that doomed their son to kill his father and marry his mother, they pinned the infant's ankles
together and left him to die. See *Oedipus the King*, 1173–
1179.

335 *busy with foot traffic* The main road north from Athens
passed through Kolonos. The implication is that Oedipus'
disclosure of his identity to the Old Men would soon be
bruited among the travelers heading toward Athens, and
that Theseus would hear it from them as he moved north.

362 *two wretched lives!* Literally, "twice-wretched." Ismene
reacts to the grim appearance of her father and sister. But
"twice-wretched" also refers to the doubling of roles, in
which his two sisters are also Oedipus' children, and thus
adds psychic wretchedness to their physical and social
misery.

371 *Those two boys imitate the Egyptians* The Greeks' cultural
norm for the division of labor between the sexes was totally

reversed in the lives of their Egyptian peers. Oedipus' sneering judgment of his sons reveals the tendency of Greeks to consider foreigners as barbarians, morally and intellectually inferior to themselves. Sophocles was possibly influenced here by the section of Herodotus' *Histories* (2.35) that documented Egyptian customs and manners.

386 *the latest oracles to your father* After Oedipus' banishment, Ismene became her father's informant—as Antigone, in a similarly helpful role, became his companion and sentinel. Ismene brought Oedipus both Theban news and oracles involving him. Since she was in effect a spy, she was living dangerously. Ismene also volunteers to perform the purification ritual required of Oedipus by the "dread goddesses," during which she's kidnapped.

398 *They were keen, at first, to let Kreon rule* The decision to allow Kreon to succeed Oedipus was prudent—both brothers realized the curse on their family might harm Thebes again, as it had during Oedipus' reign. But they changed their minds and contested the kingship, thus activating the curse. They had agreed to alternating terms. First Polyneikes ruled Thebes, but then Eteokles, who succeeded him, refused to step down, apparently with the approval of the Theban population. See note to 930.

405 *that hothead* Eteokles inherited Oedipus' impetuousness without his father's intelligence and judgment.

410 *Argos* An area in the northeastern part of the Peloponnesus.

410 *married power* After his exile from Thebes, Polyneikes' marriage to the daughter of Adrastos, king of Argos, gave him access to the Argive warrior class, which he persuaded

to lay siege to Thebes. Antigone calls her brother's marriage "deadly" (*Antigone*, 954–955) because it led to the attack that doomed both him and her.

422 *I have new oracles* It appears from the plural that Ismene has learned of two distinct oracles (probably sought by Eteokles and/or Kreon). One identified Oedipus, living or dead, as a magical defensive barrier that would protect Thebes from attack. Another promised that Oedipus himself would be transformed into a *heros* whose powers would extend beyond his physical death (see 424–435).

428 *When I'm nothing... be a man* Oedipus does not yet know he has been tapped for heroization. In the course of his next long speech (458–498), he realizes the power he's been granted and begins to wield it.

435 *Theban frontier* There were no exact, demarcated borders between Greek city-states like the ones that exist between modern contiguous countries. Thebans would therefore be making a judgment call when choosing the place near Thebes in which to hold Oedipus; it had to be far enough away so that Thebes wouldn't be contaminated by his patricidal guilt but close enough to the city to interfere with an Athenian attack force.

439 *serious trouble* The trouble might refer to the possibility of placing Oedipus' future Theban tomb in the wrong location or to some other form of neglect, such as failing to honor the dead king with libations of wine and honey.

448 *Your rage... your tomb* In their new oracles, the gods promise that Oedipus' crucial power will be manifest in his rage. The scene envisioned in this line probably refers to Oedipus' tomb should it be located in Athens. The Thebans would

deploy around it and be overwhelmed by the Athenian defenders as they fight; the dead *heros'* rage would add firepower to the attack against his former countrymen. Sophocles might allude here to the Theban raiding party that Athenian forces repulsed at Kolonos a few years before he wrote the play.

450 *Sacred envoys* Literally, *theoron*, a spectator or witness of a sacred rite or event. In this line, Sophocles specifically mentions that the envoys went to Delphi. In *Oedipus the King*, he uses the same word (*theoros*, a different grammatical case) to explain Laios' journey "into god's presence"—but he purposely withholds the king's destination. See *Oedipus the King*, note to 129–130.

450 *Delphic hearth* Apollo's oracle resided at Delphi. The hearth refers to the smoky fire that enveloped the Pythoness as she delivered her versified answer to the questions posed to her by envoys. See *Oedipus the King*, note to 1104.

458–461 *Gods, don't interfere . . . dead set* Oedipus here frames the wish that his sons both die as a request to the gods; later, at 1495–1520, he will himself deliver the same malevolence as both curse and prophecy.

464–465 *When I was driven . . . no move to stop it or help me.* At the end of *Oedipus the King*, Oedipus had asked Kreon to exile him, but Kreon refused. As implied in the *Kolonos*, Oedipus had become reconciled to Thebes and wished to remain there. Here he refers to his sons' failure to honor that wish, as well as to their dereliction of a duty fundamental in Greek law: to care for, support, and protect an aged parent.

470 *far-off day when my fury seethed* Oedipus refers to the day he became aware of the incest and patricide he had unwittingly committed—the day on which he blinded himself and

asked Kreon to banish him from Thebes. See *Oedipus the King*, 1629–1630.

489 *I recalled some prophecies* Without explaining the specifics, Oedipus makes clear that he now sees the connection between the two new prophecies brought by Ismene—that he will be transformed at death and that his dead body will have military potency—and the much earlier prophecy at Delphi, which said he would find a final home in the Eumenides' grove.

503 *Whatever my host wants done* Oedipus addresses the Leader in his specific role as adviser to strangers on the local laws and customs. As Oedipus grows more and more alienated from (and obstinate in) his relationships with his sons, the Old Men, and Kreon, he becomes increasingly acquiescent in his position as a suppliant—and he gains in divine authority.

504–531 *Ask atonement . . . If you don't . . . I'm afraid for you.* This lengthy passage, in which the Leader specifies the procedure that Oedipus, as suppliant, must follow in his ritual offering to the Eumenides, serves a dramatic purpose: Ismene, by volunteering to perform the rituals, is sent offstage long enough to be kidnapped by Kreon. But the passage also marks the beginning of Oedipus' religious involvement mentioned in the note to 503.

519 *Just pure water* The Eumenides differed from other gods because they did not receive offerings of wine. See note to 107–108.

529 *without looking back, leave* It was customary when making offerings to most gods, and especially these "dread-eyed goddesses," to avert one's eyes from the actual shrine while

pouring the offerings, to pray quietly, and then to leave the shrine "without looking back."

549–603 *Unpleasant it may be . . . ignorance* This colloquy in which the Old Men press Oedipus to confess to his incest and patricide, and during which Oedipus both admits to the facts but defends the innocence of his motives, is a choral ode and was set in the ancient productions to music and sung.

562–566 *I suffered anguish . . . I chose to do none* In this coolly rational defense of his moral innocence, Oedipus focuses on the huge imbalance between the misery he's suffered and his lack of culpability for actions he committed in ignorance. In successive restatements he will add passion to his logic, especially when replying to Kreon's accusations.

568–569 *Thebes married me . . . woman who would destroy me* The Thebans, who were grateful that Oedipus had saved them from the Sphinx, rewarded him with the throne—and Laios' widow, Jokasta, who became his wife. See introduction to *Oedipus the King*.

575 *scourges* Literally, *ata*, or "curses." Oedipus does not mean that his two much-loved daughters are literally curses, but rather that they are constant reminders of the defilement and pain his acts have caused. Speaking metaphorically, no matter how deeply they care for him, his daughters are constant scourges who pursue him in order to punish his incest and patricide. (See also note for 945–951.)

One of Theseus' Men enters I infer this stage direction to make sense of the Leader's next lines, in which he seems certain that Theseus intends to help Oedipus.

619 *I was also raised in exile* Theseus, raised by his mother
Aethra, a princess of Troezen, in the Peloponnesus, grew
up without knowing that his father was King Aigeus of
Athens. As a young man, Theseus learned the truth and
traveled to his father's home, performing many heroic feats
along the way. Similarly, Oedipus, who was raised in Kor-
inth by Polybos without knowing that his natural father
was Laios, king of Thebes, suffered great hardship after
the discovery of his true identity—and is still suffering at
this point in the play.

656 *Then what superhuman pain* do *you suffer?* Sophocles
might allude here to Oedipus' imminent transformation to
a *heros*.

661 *God's voice* The oracle. Its words, from the Pythoness of
Apollo, made clear to the Thebans that not bringing Oedipus home put their city at risk.

666–667 *All powerful / Time ravages the rest* Oedipus reminds Theseus of a lesson he first learned in *Oedipus the
King*: the only thing man can be certain of is the unstable
nature of all human relationships—including political alli-
ances between cities. Oedipus elaborates his first reference
to Time, or *Kronos*, as a teacher of acquiescence (7–8); he
now sees time as a continuum that destroys and revives
relationships. The idea is analogous to his own transformation by the gods from great king to blind beggar to honored
heros.

679–680 *Then my dead body . . . will drink their hot blood*
Oedipus extrapolates from the oracle he heard from Ismene:

that the Thebans will be defeated in battle while they are mustered near his tomb.

690 *kindness* The Greek word *eumeneia*, translated as "kindness," often refers to the goodwill of the gods. Here it echoes the name of the Eumenides, or Kindly Ones, and also alludes to a bond between Oedipus and the goddesses.

692 *our wartime ally* Some scholars, including Blundell, think this refers to a preexisting military alliance, while others, including Knox, say that it means nothing so specific or formal, but rather a traditional courtesy extended between royal houses.

697–698 *I'll settle him . . . rights of a citizen* A much-disputed line that depends upon whether one reads a Greek word at 637 in the ancient manuscripts as *empalin* or *empolin*. The line could mean respectively "*on the contrary I'll settle him in our land*" or, as I believe, and as Jebb translates, "*but will establish him as a citizen* in the land" (1886, 109). The issue is important because the granting of the highly prized Athenian citizenship rights to a foreigner like Oedipus would be a more striking demonstration of Theseus' *charis*, or grace, toward him than would his simply offering Oedipus a place to live.

728–787 *You've come, stranger . . . Nereid's skittering feet* This ode of welcome to Oedipus as an Athenian citizen touches on many visual features of the splendid Kolonian landscape. Its intent, however, is to celebrate the mythical and practical advantages for Athens inherent in these visual images. For an excellent discussion of the ode as both a hymn of praise to the pinnacle of Athens' greatness and as a requiem for the city's dying power, see Knox (1964, 154–156).

728 *shining Kolonos* The epithet "shining" may derive from the light, chalky color of Kolonos' soil, which has persisted to this day.

741–743 *Dionysos . . . maenads* Dionysos, the god associated with wine and revelry, was the son of Zeus and Semele, the daughter of Kadmos, king of Thebes. In the version of the myth adapted by Euripides in *The Bakkhai*, Semele tried to test the godliness of Zeus by challenging him to appear to her in his true shape. He did—and she was struck by lightning and thunderbolts, the symbols of his divine power. Zeus then snatched the unborn Dionysos from her body, hid him in his thigh, and took him to be brought up by nymphs, or maenads, on Mount Nysa in India. There Dionysos was schooled in the joys of wine by Silenus and the satyrs; he also cultivated a following of maenads (bacchants) who eventually traveled with him through Asia and into Greece.

749–750 *Persephone and Demeter . . . golden crocus* Demeter, the corn goddess, traveled into the underworld to find her daughter Persephone, who had been carried there (where she was forced to spend half the year) by Hades. Both goddesses are associated with death and the mysteries, which promise their initiates rebirth through the purification of death. The crocus and the nightingale also symbolize death and are fitting reminders that Oedipus will die in this grove.

751 *Bountiful . . . Kephisos* While other rivers in Attica ran dry in the summer heat, the Kephisos flowed abundantly all year.

758–759 *Goddess of Love / with golden reins in her hands*
Aphrodite, the goddess of erotic desire, was often portrayed
driving a chariot drawn by sparrows, swans, or doves.

761 *Asia* The Greeks used "Asia" to refer to what is now called
the Middle East.

761–773 *A tree not found . . . guard it with tireless glare.* Although olive trees did grow in "Asia" and the peninsula
known as Peloponnesus, the first olive tree was said to have
sprung up from the Acropolis at Athena's command. This
sacred tree, burned during the Persian wars, was also said
to have miraculously come back to life ("a tree born from
itself") and, because it was protected by Athena, to have de-
flected later invaders ("a terror to enemy spears"). "Zeus of
the Olive Groves" translates Zeus *Morios*, his title as "co-
protector" of the sacred olives. Sophocles might be using
the olive tree to symbolize more than Athens' military re-
silience and the divine protection it receives. The Athenians
believed their race was autochthonic, i.e., they were born
directly from the land. Their political system, democracy,
was similarly homegrown. The olive tree, which Sophocles
enjoins Athenian men (both young and old) not to shatter
and destroy, might symbolize the democratic institutions at
the heart of Athens' past glory.

787 *fifty Nereids* The daughters of the sea god Nereus are
sometimes portrayed escorting ships through the high seas.
Sophocles' image suggests that the Nereids' presence is vis-
ible in the rhythmic circular ripples made by the oars as they
dip into the water.

809 *fellow Kadmeans* Thebans were called Kadmeans after
Kadmos, the mythical son of Agenor and founder of Thebes.

Kadmos seeded the earth with dragon's teeth from which the Thebans grew (see *Oedipus the King*, note to 96).

819 *first vulgar lout who comes along* Kreon himself will soon live up to this description when he orders his troops to abduct Antigone and attempt to take her back to Thebes. But a darker irony in this passage harks back to *Antigone*, which Sophocles wrote some decades earlier, in which she is betrothed to Kreon's son Haimon.

834 *That would cause me unendurable pain* Oedipus knows that if he went back to Thebes, Kreon would refuse to bury his corpse; because he has committed patricide and incest, burial rites are forbidden him.

838 *you refused me* When Oedipus first pleaded to be exiled (see *Oedipus the King*, 1629–1630), Kreon refused, saying he needed first to consult the gods. Here Oedipus suggests that Kreon acted arbitrarily without such a consultation.

909 *She's mine* Oedipus asked Kreon to assume guardianship of Antigone and Ismene in *Oedipus the King*, but Antigone has hardly been under his protection, since for many years she's been wandering with Oedipus, more or less acting as his guardian.

921–922 *My city, / our city is attacked!* The issue here is not a physical attack by the Theban raiding party but the violation and abduction of Antigone, who, like Oedipus, is a suppliant under Attic protection.

927 *daughters for crutches* The word translated as crutches, *skeptroin*, literally means scepters. Blundell writes, "Since scepter is in origin a staff or walking stick, the same word in Greek is used for both. Sophocles exploits this ambiguity

to create a pathetic contrast between Oedipus' helplessness (here and at [Greek] l. 1109) and his sons' bid for the royal scepter of Thebes ([Greek] 425, 449, 1354). There is also a nice dramatic irony in [K]reon's words, since as it turns out, Oedipus will not need the support of these 'scepters' any longer" (1990, 55). At 462, 484, and 1416, I translate *skeptroin* in its singular form as "scepter," "power and a kingdom," and "your throne and your power," respectively.

930 *though I remain their king* The kingship of Thebes remains unclear throughout the play. We're told earlier that Eteokles has reneged on his agreement with Polyneikes to relinquish the throne. But does Eteokles still rule? Kreon seems to assert here that he's in power, as we assumed he would be at the end of *Oedipus the King*. See note to 398.

933–935 *turned your back . . . self-destructive fury* In *Oedipus the King*, Sophocles portrays Oedipus as full of rage and fury, a man who quickly turns in anger on his friends (especially at 760–790, where Kreon, Jokasta, and the Leader attempt to calm him down to no avail). Undoubtedly, Oedipus' two most self-destructive acts are the killing of Laios and his own self-blinding. In the *Kolonos*, Oedipus' anger loses its self-destructive power as it's transformed into a power that helps his new friends the Athenians and harms his enemies, a category that now includes both his sons.

943 *You might—unless our king stops you* Some scholars and translators attribute this line to Kreon, changing "our" to "your" as justifiably sarcastic under the circumstances.

945–951 *Goddesses . . . the curse . . . as miserable as my own* When Oedipus invokes the Eumenides in their role as guarantors of curses, he avoids calling them Kindly Ones (see 1109 and 1521). Ancient Greeks commonly cursed their enemies with the same "evils" that had been inflicted on them. The Greek word *ata* means both prayer and curse; a curse was simply a malicious or retaliatory prayer. At the end of Antigone's life, she asks that her oppressors suffer a punishment equivalent to hers (*Antigone,* 1021–1022).

949 *Let the Sun, who sees all there is* Helios, the sun god, sometimes associated with Apollo, rode a golden chariot across the sky, a perfect vantage point from which to take in everything that happens on Earth.

978 *the two I have left* At this point, having disowned his sons, he's effectively given them up as dead. Antigone will similarly treat Ismene as nonexistent after she refuses to help bury Polyneikes (*Antigone,* 95ff.).

1017 *permanent residence* Theseus makes Kreon an offer he can't refuse: bring the girls back unless he wants to be taken prisoner.

1029 *morally toxic father-killer* The Greek word translated "morally toxic" is *anagnon,* which in Jebb's words "refers to the taint of murder aggravated by union with the wife of the slain" (1886, 152). Kreon implies that Oedipus' crimes are present in his physical person and contagious. Oedipus himself agrees; at 1241 he will shrink back from his own instinctual gesture to shake Theseus' hand.

1031 *Council of Mount Ares* The ancient Athenian Council of Areopagos, which met on a hill near the Acropolis, had jurisdiction over murder and matters of impiety; it imposed penalties including fines, exile with loss of property, and death, and its judgments were final.

1048–1050 *none of which / I chose . . . whole life* Oedipus continues with increasing conviction to plead his case: because he was ignorant of the identity of his father and mother when he committed patricide and incest he believes that he is not responsible for or guilty of the crimes.

1050 *ancestors* The House of Labdakos. See note to 242–244.

1145–1202 *Oh let us . . . help this land and our people!* In this rousing ode, the Old Men imagine the action and outcome of the skirmish that ensues when Theseus and his troops set out to free Antigone and Ismene from the Thebans.

1148 *Pythian shore* The Old Men name two possible points, both on the Bay of Eleusis, where Theseus' horsemen could overtake Kreon's men, who had fled with the kidnapped daughters. The first, the "Pythian shore," would be reached via Daphni, a town in a mountain pass about six miles from Kolonos. Daphni was the site of a temple to Apollo, who is sometimes called Pythian.

1149–1154 *torch-lit beaches . . . rites for the dead* The second interception point would be at the sacred town of Eleusis, where an annual torch-lit procession was held in honor of Demeter and Persephone—the "two great queens" of the underworld (see note to 749–750). Eleusis was about five miles south of the Pythian shore. The Eleusinian rites, known as the Mysteries, were tightly guarded secrets kept from all but initiates. The priests who carried out the initiations and enforced the pledge of secrecy were always members of the family of Eumolpidae.

1162–1163 *snowy / rock in the town of Oea* The Old Men now propose a third escape route for Kreon's men. Jebb cites an ancient scholiast who identifies the "snowy rock" as an outcrop of Mount Aigaleos near the Athenian rural district or *deme* of Oea, several miles northwest of Kolonos (1886, 1059n).

1172 *Athena* Athena, also a goddess of horses, shared an altar at Kolonos with Poseidon, presumably the altar where Theseus has been making sacrifices.

1175 *goddess Rhea* Poseidon was the son of Kronos and Rhea.

1198–1199 *Apollo, / bring Artemis* Apollo, the god whose weapon of choice was the bow and arrow, was the brother of Artemis, the goddess of hunting.

1294–1316 *Father, please hear me . . . repay it.* Antigone's substantial speech is noteworthy in several respects. It demonstrates her intense sisterly concern for Polyneikes. In asking her father to show compassion, she invokes the damage the family curse has inflicted by having parents punish their children. Antigone fears that Oedipus' cruelty will affect others besides Polyneikes. She's right; Oedipus' rejection of Polyneikes will have a role in Antigone's own death.

1326–1369 *Anyone who craves . . . northern mountains* In this starkly unsentimental and keenly detailed picture of aging, the Old Men remind the audience of an implied alternative to accepting one's painful final years. Death and the ultimate home of the dead, Hades, become a wished-for release. The outlook resembles that of Hamlet's "To be or not to be" soliloquy.

1344–1350 *By any measure . . . place he came from* The sentiments in this famously pessimistic Greek proverb—the story
goes back at least to the archaic period—belong to Silenus,
the leader of the satyrs in Dionysos' band of revelers. When
asked (while drunk), "What's best?" he answered, "Never
to be born at all." Second best, if one was unlucky enough to
be born, was to go back wherever one came from as quickly
as possible. Easterling (52–53) writes, "Death never ceased
to be a defining feature of tragedy in Greek tradition; it is
perhaps not an accident that the presiding deity of the festivals which included tragedy [i.e., Dionysos] should have
such strong connexions with the world of the dead." See the
introduction passim for examples of the Dionysiac influence
on Athens' great theater festival.

1389 *Respect* In the Greek, *aidos*. Many scholars and translators use "Mercy" here, but I follow Blundell in interpret-
ing Respect as the goddess that Polyneikes personifies as an
attendant of Zeus (1990). The tenor of Polyneikes' speech
suggests that he is appealing precisely for respect rather than
begging for mercy. Oedipus counters and rejects Polyneikes'
invocation by personifying Justice as Zeus' attendant at
1508.

1395 *Will you deny me with silent contempt?* As a suppliant,
Polyneikes is due the honor of an answer to a request, but
as both Theseus and Antigone explain, at 1291–1293 and
1294–1316, Oedipus is not bound to grant the request.
Oedipus might be silent for the moment, but he unleashes
his wrath at 1480ff.

1415–1416 *elder son . . . to inherit your throne* Since primogeniture was not customary in ancient Greece, Polyneikes' argument loses some of its force.

1420 *persuaded Thebes to back him* Polyneikes implies that Eteokles manipulated the Thebans into backing him—a tactic, writes Blundell, that democrats in Sophocles' time would have approved of (1990, 139n). The word literally translated as persuade, *peisas*, often euphemistically connotes bribery, writes Knox (1982, 1467n).

1421–1422 *the Fury who stalks you / strengthened his case* Polyneikes, with characteristic tactlessness, blames the ancient curse on Oedipus for the quarrel between the brothers.

1428–1429 *seven companies / of spearmen to fight Thebes* Polyneikes has convinced six Argive warlords to join his attack on the seven gates of Thebes and put him back in power. They will not succeed. Here Polyneikes presents his strategy for the assault, presumably hoping for his father's approval. The most colorful of the seven participants are noted below. Also see *Antigone*, note to line 20.

1435 *Amphiaraos* Amphiaraos, once the king of Argos, was a seer who refused to take part in the ill-fated siege against Thebes until his wife Eriphyle shamed him to join the battle. (Polyneikes had bribed her to do so with a golden heirloom necklace that belonged to his family.)

1441 *Kapaneus* Kapaneus, who boasted that nothing could stop him from scaling the walls of Thebes to set its houses on fire, was struck down for his arrogance by a thunderbolt from Zeus. See *Antigone*, 148ff.

1444 *Atalanta* Atalanta, the late-life mother of Parthenopaios, was disowned by her father and raised in the woods by a she-bear in Arcadia. She swore never to marry unless the successful suitor outran her in a footrace. In some versions of the myth, Milanion, who fathered her son, met Atalanta's conditions by dropping three golden apples along the route of a race, each of which she stopped to pick up. He thereby overtook her.

1457 *fountains of home* Springs, the source of fresh water essential for life, were considered symbolic of the land and often protected by nymphs.

1459–1460 *I'm a beggar . . . but so are you* Polyneikes overlooks a crucial difference between Oedipus' status as beggar and exile and his own: Oedipus brings with him a helpful "gift" for his benefactor; Polyneikes only pleads for help.

1498–1499 *The blood you shed will defile you . . . as he dies* Oedipus means that the brothers will defile each other by committing simultaneous fratricide.

1500–1522 *I cursed you both . . . Ares the Destroyer* Oedipus imagines his curses (in the Greek, *arai*) almost as having physical force. He speaks of them as allies, as fellow fighters in his campaign to teach his sons to respect their parents. Jebb writes, "The *arai,* when they have once passed the father's lips, are henceforth personal agencies of vengeance" (1886, 1375n). Tartaros is the part of the underworld where evildoers are punished for their crimes. The native spirits Oedipus summons are the Eumenides in their punitive mode.

1508 *Justice* Oedipus responds to Polyneikes' personification of Respect at 1389 by invoking Justice, a goddess who can be expected to carry out Zeus' will without mitigation.

1538–1539 *don't dishonor me ... Perform the rituals* In *Antigone*, she will honor her brother by performing the burial rites he requests, but by doing so she risks her own life.

1580–1628 *We've just seen ... Zeus!* In this choral ode, the gods begin their final and benign intervention in Oedipus' life. The heightened musical energy from song and wind instruments accompanies Oedipus' understanding and acceptance that he is being called to his death.

1594 *That was thunder! O Zeus!* In Apollo's original oracle, thunder and lightning were two of the three signs that would announce Oedipus' death and transformation.

1652 *My life is weighted to sink down* This ancient image is of a balance scale in which Zeus decides the outcome of life-or-death matters by weighting the scale so that it sinks the doomed person or people.

1698 *Hermes* As the messenger of Zeus, one of Hermes' duties was to escort the souls of the dead to the underworld.

1708 *unseen goddess* Persephone, queen of the underworld, was called the unseen goddess, perhaps because her husband's name, Hades, literally means "unseen."

1711 *Aidoneus* Aidoneus is a longer version of Hades' name. The Old Men address him tentatively because he is notoriously resistant to prayer. See *Antigone*, 857, where Kreon makes a jibe at Antigone by snidely suggesting she pray to Hades to save her life.

1715 *house of Styx* A reference to the River Styx that runs through the underworld.

1719 *Earth Goddesses!* The Eumenides.

1721 *Savage guard-dog!* Cerberus, the monstrous three-headed dog who stands guard at the entrance to the underworld, was said to be docile to those who entered but to devour all who attempted to leave.

1743 *steep brass steps* See note to 65.

1744 *a maze of crossing paths* This might allude to the crossroads where Oedipus killed Laios and to the maze of fated events in his life.

1746–1747 *immortal pact that Theseus / made with Peirithous* Before attempting to rescue Persephone from the underworld, Theseus and his friend Peirithous pledged their everlasting friendship at a place "where a bowl had been hollowed from a rock shelf." But Hades trapped and detained them both. In most versions of the myth, Herakles rescued Theseus but left Peirithous to suffer the torments of the criminal dead.

1748–1750 *rock / of Thoricos . . . stone tomb* These local landmarks (and their significance) would have been familiar to Sophocles' audience. Although the exact location of the spot where Oedipus is transformed must remain a secret, the detailed geographical description adds credibility to the miraculous destination of Oedipus' final journey.

1758–1759 *washed . . . white clothes customary* Literally, "gave him the bath and the prescribed clothing." Greek burial rituals included washing the corpse and dressing it in white garments. See *Antigone* introduction.

1762 *Zeus of the Underworld thundered* A reference to Hades. Both Hades and the Olympian Zeus are the supreme gods of their respective realms below and above the Earth. The earthquake is the third and last of the signs that Apollo told Oedipus would signal his imminent death.

1778 *enormous voice called him* Blundell suggests that the god who beckons Oedipus might be identified with Hermes, Persephone, or perhaps Hades himself (1990, 190n), but the anonymity of the god's voice adds to the mystery.

1818–1820 *Earth's lower world . . . welcoming kindness* For a discussion of this passage, see *Kolonos* introduction, pp. 500–501.

1924–1925 *the Earth Powers / have shown us all so much grace* Theseus reminds the grieving Antigone and Ismene that by allowing their father to die a painless death in this sacred grove, the gods of Hades have blessed both Oedipus and Athens.

1936 *Horkos* The son of Eris, or Strife. His role is to witness and enforce oaths, and therefore to end contention and war by bringing mortals together in binding agreements.

WORKS CITED AND CONSULTED

Aeschylus. *The Complete Greek Tragedies*. Trans. Richmond Lattimore, ed. David Grene and Richmond Lattimore. Chicago: University of Chicago Press, 1959.

Aristotle. *Aristotle's Poetics*. Trans. Leon Golden. Tallahassee: Florida State University Press, 1981.

——. *The Art of Rhetoric*. Trans. John Henry Freese. Loeb Classical Library 193. Cambridge, MA: Harvard University Press, 1967.

Berlin, Normand. *The Secret Cause: A Discussion of Tragedy*. Amherst: University of Massachusetts Press, 1981.

Blundell, Mary Whitlock. *Helping Friends and Harming Enemies: A Study in Sophocles and Greek Ethics*. Cambridge: Cambridge University Press, 1989.

——, trans. *Oedipus at Colonus*. By Sophocles. Focus Classical Library. Newburyport, MA: Focus Information Group, 1990.

Boegehold, Alan L. *When a Gesture Was Expected*. Princeton, NJ: Princeton University Press, 1999.

Carpenter, Thomas H., and Christopher A. Faraone, eds. *Masks of Dionysus*. Ithaca, NY: Cornell University Press, 1993.

Cartledge, Paul. *Ancient Greek Political Thought in Practice*. Cambridge: Cambridge University Press, 2009.

Csapo, Eric. *Actors and Icons of the Ancient Theater.* West Sussex, UK: Wiley-Blackwell, 2000.

Csapo, Eric, and William J. Slater. *The Context of Ancient Drama.* Ann Arbor: University of Michigan Press, 1994.

Davidson, John N. *Courtesans and Fishcakes: The Consuming Passions of Classical Athens.* New York: St. Martin's Press, 1998.

Easterling, P. E., ed. *The Cambridge Companion to Greek Tragedy.* Cambridge: Cambridge University Press, 1997.

Edmunds, Lowell. *Theatrical Space and Historical Place in Sophocles' "Oedipus at Colonus."* Lanham, MD: Rowman & Littlefield, 1996.

Else, Gerald F. *The Origin and Early Form of Greek Tragedy.* New York: Norton, 1965.

Euripides. *Euripides.* The Complete Greek Tragedies, vol. 4. Ed. David Grene and Richmond Lattimore. Chicago: University of Chicago Press, 1959.

Foley, Helene P. *Female Acts in Greek Tragedy.* Princeton, NJ: Princeton University Press, 2001.

Garland, Robert. *The Greek Way of Death.* Ithaca, NY: Cornell University Press, 1985.

——. *The Greek Way of Life.* Ithaca, NY: Cornell University Press, 1990.

Goldhill, Simon. *Reading Greek Tragedy.* Cambridge: Cambridge University Press, 1986.

Goldhill, Simon, and Edith Hall. *Sophocles and the Greek Tragic Tradition.* Cambridge: Cambridge University Press, 2000.

Gould, Thomas. *The Ancient Quarrel Between Poetry and Philosophy.* Princeton, NJ: Princeton University Press, 1990.

————, trans. *"Oedipus the King": A Translation with Commentary*. By Sophocles. Englewood Cliffs, NJ: Prentice-Hall, 1970.

Grene, David, trans. *Sophocles 1*. 2nd ed. The Complete Greek Tragedies. Ed. David Grene and Richmond Lattimore. Chicago: University of Chicago Press, 1991.

Guthrie, W. K. C. *The Greeks and Their Gods*. Boston: Beacon Press, 1950.

Hanson, Victor Davis. *A War Like No Other*. New York: Random House, 2005.

Herodotus. *The Landmark Herodotus: The Histories*. Ed. Robert B. Strassler. New York: Pantheon Books, 2007.

Hughes, Bettany. *The Hemlock Cup: Socrates, Athens and the Search for the Good Life*. New York: Knopf, 2010.

Jebb, R. C., trans. *Oedipus Coloneus*. By Sophocles. Cambridge: Cambridge University, 1886.

Kagan, Donald. *Pericles of Athens and the Birth of Democracy*. New York: Touchstone–Simon & Schuster, 1991.

Kirkwood, G. M. *A Study of Sophoclean Drama*. Cornell Studies in Classical Philology 31. Ithaca, NY: Cornell University Press, 1994.

Knox, Bernard M. W. *Essays: Ancient and Modern*. Baltimore: Johns Hopkins University Press, 1989.

————. *The Heroic Temper: Studies in Sophoclean Tragedy*. Berkeley: University of California Press, 1964.

————. *Oedipus at Thebes*. New Haven, CT: Yale University Press, 1957.

————. Introduction and notes to *The Three Theban Plays*. By Sophocles. Trans. Robert Fagles. New York: Viking, 1982.

Lefkowitz, Mary R. *The Lives of Greek Poets*. Baltimore: Johns Hopkins University Press, 1981.

Lloyd-Jones, Hugh, trans. *Oedipus at Colonus*. By Sophocles. Loeb Classical Library 21. Cambridge, MA: Harvard University Press, 1994.

Lloyd-Jones, Hugh, and N. G. Wilson. *Hypomnemata*. Göttingen, Germany: Vandenhoeck & Ruprecht, 1997.

———. *Sophoclea: Studies on the Text of Sophocles*. Oxford: Clarendon Press, 1990.

Moore, J. A., trans. *Selections from the Greek Elegiac, Iambic, and Lyric Poets*. Cambridge, MA: Harvard University Press, 1947.

Pickard-Cambridge, Arthur. *The Dramatic Festivals of Athens*. 2nd ed. Revised with a new supplement by John Gould and D. M. Lewis. Oxford: Clarendon Press, 1988.

Plutarch. *The Rise and Fall of Athens: Nine Greek Lives*. Trans. Ian Scott-Kilvert. London: Penguin, 1960.

Radice, Betty. *Who's Who in the Ancient World*. London: Penguin, 1971.

Rehm, Rush. *The Play of Space: Spatial Transformation in Greek Tragedy*. Princeton, NJ: Princeton University Press, 2002.

Reinhardt, Karl. *Sophocles*. New York: Barnes & Noble–Harper & Row, 1979.

Seaford, Richard. *Reciprocity and Ritual: Homer and Tragedy in the Developing City-State*. Oxford: Clarendon Press, 1994.

Segal, Charles. *Sophocles' Tragic World: Divinity, Nature, Society*. Cambridge, MA: Harvard University Press, 1995.

———. *Tragedy and Civilization: An Interpretation of Sophocles.* Cambridge, MA: Harvard University Press, 1981.

Taplin, Oliver. *Greek Tragedy in Action.* Berkeley: University of California Press, 1978.

Thucydides. *The Landmark Thucydides: A Comprehensive Guide to the Peloponnesian War.* Ed. Robert B. Strassler. New York: Touchstone–Simon & Schuster, 1996.

Vernant, Jean-Pierre, ed. *The Greeks.* Trans. Charles Lambert and Teresa Lavender Fagan. Chicago: University of Chicago Press, 1995.

Vernant, Jean-Pierre, and Pierre Vidal-Naquet. *Myth and Tragedy in Ancient Greece.* Trans. Janet Lloyd. New York: Zone Books, 1990.

Whitman, C. E. *Sophocles.* Cambridge, MA: Harvard University Press, 1951.

Wiles, David. *Greek Theatre Performances: An Introduction.* Cambridge: Cambridge University Press, 2000.

———. *Tragedy in Athens: Performance Space and Theatrical Meaning.* Cambridge: Cambridge University Press, 1997.

Winkler, John J., and Froma I. Zeitlin, eds. *Nothing to Do with Dionysos?: Athenian Drama in Its Social Context.* Princeton, NJ: Princeton University Press, 1990.

Winnington-Ingram, R. P. *Sophocles: An Interpretation.* Cambridge: Cambridge University Press, 1980.

Zimmern, Alfred. *The Greek Commonwealth: Politics and Economics in Fifth-Century Greece.* 5th ed. New York: Modern Library, 1931.

ACKNOWLEDGMENTS

Translation is a thoroughly collaborative venture. The many scholars, theater practitioners, and friends who read and commented on this work at various stages deserve gratitude.

Three classicists, Thomas Fauss Gould, John Andrew Moore, and Charles Segal, did not live to see the publication of the present volume, but their influence and advice remains in the translations, introductions, and notes to the three Oedipus plays.

Mary Bagg's editing of the notes to this volume gave them clarity and accuracy they would not otherwise possess.

Thanks to the following readers for their contributions and suggestions: Normand Berlin, Michael Birtwistle, Alan L. Boegehold, Donald Junkins, Tracy Kidder, Robin Magowan, William Mullen, Arlene and James Scully, and Richard Trousdell.

Special thanks to my agent, Wendy Strothman, who saw the possibility of a complete volume of Sophocles and skillfully helped accomplish it.

ABOUT THE TRANSLATOR

Robert Bagg is a graduate of Amherst College (1957). He received his PhD in English from the University of Connecticut (1965) and taught at the University of Washington (1963–65) and the University of Massachusetts, Amherst (1965–96), where he served as Graduate Director (1982–86) and Department Chair (1986–92). His awards include grants from the American Academy of Arts and Letters, the Ingram Merrill Foundation, the NEA and NEH, and the Guggenheim and Rockefeller foundations. His translations of Greek drama have been staged in sixty productions on three continents. Bagg, who is writing a critical biography of Richard Wilbur, lives in western Massachusetts with his wife, Mary Bagg, a freelance writer and editor.

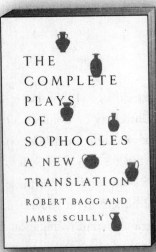
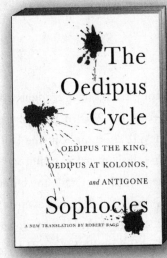